Strengthening the States

Strengthening the States

ESSAYS ON LEGISLATIVE REFORM

edited by

DONALD G. HERZBERG
ALAN ROSENTHAL

Doubleday & Company, Inc., Garden City, New York

1971

LIBRARY OF CONGRESS CATALOG CARD NUMBER 78-157600
COPYRIGHT © 1971 BY RUTGERS—THE STATE UNIVERSITY
ALL RIGHTS RESERVED
PRINTED IN THE UNITED STATES OF AMERICA
FIRST EDITION

Preface

We live in an era of crisis and change—one that will witness either the decline or the improvement of life, either the demise or the renaissance of state governments and state legislatures. We believe that the well-being of the states and the health of the nation are inextricably linked. This volume of essays reflects our belief. It is dedicated to the proposition that if state government is to be strengthened, state legislatures must be improved.

For three decades centralization dominated the American system. The states abdicated responsibility; but the federal government cannot shoulder it alone. Despite national commitments, major problems are unsolved, urgent needs are unmet. Perhaps as a consequence, today the thrust is toward greater decentralization and increased participation at all levels of government. There is a recognition—rooted in the past, and re-emerging forcefully in the present—that the states must play a vital role if the nation and its people are to survive and prosper.

Grave problems confront all of us: the deterioration of the environment, substandard housing, unemployment and underemployment, rising crime and violence, the inadequacies of educational systems, poverty and sickness, and the crises of race and social class. The states must face these problems. Coping with them, let alone solving them, demands independent creativity, a diversity of approach, widespread involvement, intense participation, and the will to persist, however difficult or discouraging the job.

I

Too often the states have relied on their governors and administrative bureaucracies to decide and do what had to be done. This cannot suffice, for a concentration of power in one branch of government is no more satisfactory than a concentration of power at one level of government.

Checks and balances, we believe, is more than a notion willed us by our Federalist forefathers. It is a necessary principle to follow if government is to be representative and effective. The executive branch, whatever its popularity, capability, or good faith, may commit errors. The legislature should be there to remedy them. Tyranny is probably no danger, but the executive may occasionally do wrong. The legislature must be there to right it. Frequently, the executive is weak or unimaginative, unwilling or unable to act. It then falls to the legislature to provide leadership.

With the growth of the size and complexity of government, the legislature must not only balance its governor, it must also check the administrators in the departments and agencies of the executive branch. These people, as much as elected politicians, have tremendous impact on state policies and programs and on citizens' lives. Specialists and technicians—like all of us, governors and governed—make mistakes. Some stem from faulty reasoning, some from foolishness, and some from vested interests in programs. Some occur because the values, assumptions, and perspectives of specialists and technicians are not shared by the people affected by their decisions.

State legislatures, with few exceptions, require strengthening as political institutions. Otherwise they will not be independent of governors, of executive departments and agencies, of political party and factional organizations, of special interests. Otherwise they will not play a significant part in the governance of the states. State legislatures, without exception, require improvement as political institutions. Otherwise they will never become real forums, where new needs are expressed, where all issues are faced, and where innovations are given life.

The future of the state legislature depends on its ability to perform three types of tasks.

First, the legislature must participate vigorously in policy making. It cannot merely ratify proposals—whether an executive budget, departmental request, or member's bill. It has to attend to the trivial (for what is trivial to many is important to a few), and yet examine every important item thoroughly. It has to deliberate thoughtfully, and still encourage the expression of different viewpoints and clashing interests. It should be able to change, modify, or reject what is presented; and it must be able to offer alternatives and fill in the gaps left by an administration's program.

Second, the legislature must review and evaluate the conduct of administration and the effects of state programs. It cannot merely abandon enactments to the executive branch, on the assumption that its job is completed once a bill becomes law. It has to check continuously whether departments and agencies are operating efficiently, whether they are performing effectively. It must determine the effects programs have, and at just what costs. Only then can the legislature decide, more sensibly than before, on reducing some programs and abandoning others, on expanding in one domain and making a new start in another.

Third, the legislature must represent and help out constituents. This means that legislators not only have to do errands for people, put them in touch with administrators, answer their requests, and even express their interests. It means also that legislators have to respond to the needs as well as the preferences of people, and explain to them how and why.

II

The objective of a strong, competent legislature is not an easy one to achieve. Nor does the history of state legislatures provide great encouragement. As recently as 1966, Alexander Heard, chancellor of Vanderbilt University, commented harshly:

> State legislatures may be our most extreme example of institutional lag. In their formal qualities they are largely nineteenth-century organizations and they must, or should, address themselves to twentieth-century problems.

This is not an epitaph, however. In the few years since Heard wrote, the signs of legislative resurgence have been remarkable.

Nearly all state legislatures have become aware of the benefits of institutional change. Many have accepted the necessity for substantial improvement. A large number have demonstrated the will to take positive action. Today, the movement toward reform is well under way. There can be no guarantees; but if the most recent past is prologue, then state legislatures have a decent chance in the future.

Legislatures must take the initiative. National organizations composed of legislator members—notably the National Legislative Conference (NLC) and the National Conference of State Legislative Leaders (NCSLL)—play an important role too. People on the outside are also taking a part. Individuals, businesses, universities, and foundations are contributing energy and funds in the belief that state legislatures can be changed and revitalized.

A major vehicle for reform is the Citizens Conference on State Legislatures (CCSL), which was founded in 1965 and which has its headquarters in Kansas City, Missouri. Its record in working with private citizens and public officials throughout the nation to improve state legislatures is a distinguished one. CCSL has helped organize and then collaborated with state citizen commissions; developed a series of conferences for representatives of the news media; sponsored surveys of voters on matters of legislative reform; distributed widely educational materials in state legislatures and institutional change; participated in organizing and running seminars for legislative leaders; conducted a program to inform the public and increase its awareness of the need for legislative improvement; and completed a massive study evaluating the fifty state legislatures, on the basis of their functionality, accountability, information-handling capacity, independence, and representativeness.

The Eagleton Institute of Politics at Rutgers University is another group that has tried to help state legislatures help themselves. Since its establishment in 1956, the Eagleton Institute has engaged in numerous programs, all of which entailed either education in government and politics, research on government and politics, or the application of knowledge to the solution of public problems.

Only a few years ago, Eagleton became particularly concerned with state legislatures, which we felt had become weak links in the chains connecting public policy with citizen needs and demands. The impetus for us to translate our concern into action was Jess Unruh, then speaker of the California Assembly. His commitment and the logic of his argument were most welcome at Eagleton, where he served as a visiting lecturer. In 1965–66 the Institute really began to involve itself with state legislatures. It became the research and development arm of the National Conference of State Legislative Leaders and it created a Center for State Legislative Research and Service. In the brief period since then, our activities with regard to legislatures have been varied. Chief among them are studies, which have been commissioned by seven legislatures, and annual conferences, which have been attended by state legislators from throughout the nation.

III

The essays appearing in this volume are the result of Eagleton's conferences for state legislators.

Funded by the Carnegie Corporation and held each summer
since 1966, these week-long meetings have been at Key Biscayne,
Naples, and Marco Island, all in Florida. Two outstanding
legislators from each of the sixteen most populous states were
invited to the first two conferences. The next three were expanded
to include two outstanding legislators from each of twenty-
five states, with half of the states represented one summer and
the other half the next. During the period from 1966 through
1970, over two hundred members from the houses and senates
of forty-nine states attended.

In bringing together the most capable legislators and placing
them in an environment where they can share legislative problems and prospects, our intention has been twofold. We hoped
to inform them about the possibility and potential of change.
We hoped also to encourage them to persuade one another
and their colleagues back home of their stakes in institutional
reform. It is difficult, of course, to evaluate the extent to which
the objectives of the program have been fulfilled, but we feel
that something substantial has been accomplished.

We had to have as participants members who would remain
in office long enough to exercise the influence required to impel
their legislatures toward reform. In this, we have been fortunate.
Nationwide, the average turnover in legislative membership is
about 30 percent. Yet attrition in our group has been only
about half that figure. Among the 116 who attended the first
three sessions, nearly one hundred are still serving in their legislatures. Over a third of them had achieved positions of leadership
—as chairman of an appropriations, finance, or ways and means
committee, as majority or minority leader or assistant leader,

as president or president pro tem of the senate, as speaker of the house.

We had to have as participants members who were dedicated and able enough to do the job. Here, too, we were fortunate. Upon returning to their legislatures, many of those who had attended a conference got to work on reform quickly. The comments of a few legislators from various states are illustrative:

> Much of what we learned at Key Biscayne is beginning to bear fruit in this state. The legislature will go into special session later this month to begin revising the constitution, and a study committee will attempt modernization of the legislative process.

> As a result of our discussions on conflicts of interest at the seminar in 1967, I drafted two bills which became effective as laws in September 1968.

> We are one month into our current session and I believe that both Representative ———— and myself are finding our experience at Eagleton extremely productive. Representative ———— was elected majority whip and we are both talking to our colleagues with regard to legislative reform.

> I like to think that I had something to do with the prospects of the district office, for immediately upon returning from your conference in 1967 I forwarded a letter with an outline of the California system to ————, the Senate minority leader. He later informed me he sent it along to Majority Leader ————. Perhaps this small advance toward greater service by legislators . . . is a direct result of the Eagleton Institute's conference.

> As a consequence of my attending the Key Biscayne conference, I have proposed a number of changes in our procedure, some of which are outlined in the enclosed draft of an article I wrote.

> As a result of enthusiasm for legislative improvement generated by my attendance at the Institute, I promoted a salary increase at the last session. . . . Current improvement efforts are aimed at getting some kind of adequate office space.

Two remarkable cases of legislative improvement may in small part at least be traced to seeds sown at the Florida conferences. Participants from Ohio returned to their state, and in short order transformed one house of the legislature. In Florida greater progress has been made during the last few years than most states have made in decades. Accomplishments by the Florida legislature cannot be attributed to Eagleton's annual conferences, but we like to believe that the attendance of six of its outstanding members did make a difference.

IV

At Eagleton's five conferences, about thirty papers, prepared by governors, legislators, and other experts, have been presented at plenary sessions and then discussed at daily workshops. Sixteen of the essays in this book are based on these papers, which have been revised by the authors. Two others were presented to legislative leaders at a November 1969 conference, sponsored jointly by NCSLL, CCSL, and Eagleton. Several of these essays have been published in somewhat different form in annual issues of the Yearbook of the National Conference of State Legislative Leaders.

The sixteen individuals whose essays appear here include:

Four men who have served as governor of their states: Harold E. Hughes of Iowa; Richard B. Ogilvie of Illinois; Carl E. Sanders of Georgia; and Warren P. Knowles of Wisconsin;

Four men who have worked on behalf of reform within the legislature: Jess Unruh of California; Charles F. Kurfess of Ohio; Robert P. Knowles of Wisconsin; and Harold A. Katz of Illinois;

Four political scientists who have studied legislatures and legislative reform: Duane Lockard from Princeton University; William J. Keefe from the University of Pittsburgh; Howard Penniman from Georgetown University; and Alan Rosenthal from Rutgers University; and

Four others who have been closely involved with legislatures and legislative reform: Howard R. Sacks, dean of the University of Connecticut Law School; Arthur Bolton, former director of the California Assembly's Office of Research; Larry Margolis, executive director of CCSL; and Charles O. Davis, executive secretary of NCSLL.

This volume is organized into three sections, each of which includes a general introduction covering the area as well as the essays. Part One, "The Scope of Legislative Reform," deals with the rationale and proposals central to the movement. Part Two, "The Views of Executive and Legislative Leaders," presents the opinions and programs of the men who have had first-hand experience. Part Three, "Strategies and Tactics of Reform," considers obstacles and opportunities, and shows how improvement can be accomplished. At the end of the volume, there is a selected bibliography that describes and lists some of the most useful publications on the subjects of state legislatures and legislative reform.

v

We, the editors, are proud to participate in the movement for state legislative reform. Whatever royalties derive from the sale of this book will be used to support the activities of Eagleton's Center for State Legislative Research and Service.

The many individuals and groups with whom we have participated have earned our gratitude. Our debt to Jess Unruh is so huge that it can never be repaid. The efforts of Raymond Bateman, Ross Cunningham, William J. Keefe, Evron Kirkpatrick, Robert P. Knowles, Thomas Littlewood, and Bernard Ruggieri, all of whom served as members of the advisory committee for the state legislator conferences, are greatly appreciated.

Two hundred legislators and others who participated in the Florida conferences also deserve our thanks. Without them, legislative reform would be a shadow of what it is today. We owe much to Larry Margolis of CCSL and Charles O. Davis of NCSLL, with whom we have collaborated these past years.

We probably owe even more to the Carnegie Corporation, which funded all of the conferences, and to the Ford Foundation, which funded much of the Eagleton Institute.

And at Eagleton our debts continue to pile up. We are grateful to Wendy Ashmore, Chickie Charwin, Pat DeCandia, Juanda Kirk, Karen Osowski, John and Sally Runyon, Edith Saks, and Chris Shaw, all of whom in one way or another helped prepare this book for publication.

We are especially thankful for having known and worked with Mason Gross. He was a key participant in the Florida conferences and is retiring after twelve years as president of Rutgers. All of us who have enjoyed the pleasure of his company and the benefit of his leadership will miss him.

DONALD G. HERZBERG

ALAN ROSENTHAL

New Brunswick, New Jersey
April 1971

Contents

part one

THE SCOPE OF LEGISLATIVE REFORM

The Scope of Legislative Reform
An Introduction

ALAN ROSENTHAL

If state legislatures are in need of improvement, the first question to ask is what kind of improvement is necessary. For the past two decades, since the American Political Science Association set up a committee on American legislatures, this question has been asked with increasing frequency. Expert consultants, political scientists, concerned citizens, and politicians themselves have diagnosed legislative ailments and prescribed remedies. Diagnosis and prescription have been reiterated time and time again —by the National Legislative Conference, by the American Assembly and its regional assemblies, by the Citizens Conference on State Legislatures, by the Eagleton Institute of Politics, and by numerous other groups and organizations.

I

It is remarkable, in fact, how ideas of legislative improvement have carried over virtually intact. These extremely durable ideas constitute the contemporary agenda for reform. Although variously phrased and differently stressed, depending on time, place, and source, the program includes the following items.

1. Elimination of many constitutional limitations on the authority of state legislatures, including limits on the taxing power, earmarking of revenues, requirements on referenda, and legislator compensation.

2. Increase in the frequency and length of legislative sessions, without limitation of time or subject.

3. Reduction of the size of legislative bodies, so that they are no larger than fair representation requires.

4. Increase in compensation and related benefits, with expenses of legislative service fully reimbursed.

5. The adoption of more rigorous standards of conduct, by means of codes of ethics and conflict of interest, disclosure, and lobbying legislation, as well as ethics committees or commissions with some enforcement powers.

6. Adequate space and facilities for committees and individual members, including electronic data processing and roll-call voting equipment.

7. Improvement of legislative operations, to ensure efficiency in the consideration of bills and the widespread dissemination of procedural and substantive information.

8. Strengthening of standing committees, by reducing their number, defining their jurisdictions, and improving their procedures.

9. Increasing the number and competence of legislative staff, including staff for the leadership, committees, and rank-and-file members.

Proposals such as these are discussed in a number of essays that appear throughout the volume. In this part, Larry Margolis, the executive director of the Citizens Conference, makes a strong case for the adoption of many of the reforms. He notes that practically every study of a legislature arrives at approximately the same results, and thus the same items keep reappearing on the agenda. In any case, he points out that the purpose of studies by legislators, citizens, or consultants "is not so much to discover what is wrong with the legislature or what the legislature needs, but rather to carry public opinion along in support of the recommendations that will inevitably result." No one claims that a general reform program perfectly fits each state in the Union. Each, of course, is different, and consequently the particular problems and specific needs of one legislature might be quite unlike those of another. Some contemporary legislatures—such as those in California, Florida, Hawaii, and Wisconsin—are rather highly developed institutions. Whatever their ailments, the remedies for them are unlikely to be found among the general and convenient lists that have been compiled in the past. By contrast, some legislatures—such as ones in Alabama, Mississippi, New Hampshire, New Jersey, and Wyoming—are still rather underdeveloped. The reforms mentioned above are not at all inappropriate as a starting point for their efforts toward improvement.

II

Perhaps, as many assert, it is not the institutions of the political system that pose the problem, but rather the men who run them. The states have certainly had their share of difficulties in this respect. The situation today is far better than in the latter half of the nineteenth century, when popular discontent with the quality of legislatures and legislators reached a zenith. Yet, it is still hard to attract and then hold the most able men in legislative service. Turnover in state legislatures is high, more than twice as high as in the U. S. Congress. After an average election, perhaps one-third of the members are replaced by newcomers. Nor is it certain that the best members make the legislature their career or stay long enough to make a real difference.

The "lawmakers," to use James David Barber's term, are

those who are active, attend to substantive tasks, and make the most significant contributions. They are too few in number, and their future in the legislature depends on competing demands for their talents. Some run for statewide office, others seek seats in the U. S. Congress, and a few return full-time to their private careers. One of my acquaintances, for example, a lawmaker highly regarded by his leaders, his colleagues, his constituents, and the press, simply could not stand the frustration of pursuing two careers. A lawyer, he felt he could neither fully meet his responsibilities to the legislature nor to his profession, firm, and clients. Thus, he decided to choose a single career. He entered a primary race contesting and then winning a seat held by an incumbent in the U. S. House of Representatives. After only four years his service in the state legislature is at an end; it will not be easy to fill his place.

Problems such as these—and what can be done about them—are the concern of Duane Lockard, who served briefly in the Connecticut Senate and is now in the politics department at Princeton University. In his essay, exploring how a legislative career can be made attractive, Lockard shows that the caliber of men is linked, at least indirectly, to the nature of the institution. Members, he suggests, leave the legislature because of inadequate compensation, poor facilities, clumsy legislative methods, and the conflict-of-interest situation in which they inevitably find themselves. In order to increase member incentives to continue in service, he recommends higher salaries and better facilities, annual and longer sessions, and greater order in legislative operations.

What the institution owes its members in the way of tangible rewards is one side of the coin; the other side, of course, is what members owe not only the institution but also the constituents whom they serve. Simply stated, legislators as public officials must observe high standards of ethics and conduct, regardless of pressures or opportunities to do otherwise. Because of the nature of political life, especially the costs of campaigning, the variety of issues with which politicians must deal, and the necessity to compromise, it is understandable that ethics pose a challenge. There have been—and will continue to be—scandals in the U. S. Congress, where members are full-time and adequately compensated. The dilemma in the state legislature is even more serious; here service is part-time, and the member must earn a substantial portion of his livelihood on the outside.

Howard Sacks, dean of the University of Connecticut Law School, has devoted considerable attention to ethical problems confronting the state legislator, notably as a member of the Illinois Conflict of Interest Laws Commission. In his essay, he discusses these problems and makes suggestions for dealing with them. Sacks treats a number of matters central to any consideration of legislator ethics: financial interests of members in state contracts; bribery; rewards for official action; lobbying for compensation; privately financed expense funds; member interests in legislative issues; representation of private clients in matters before state agencies; and the enforcement of adopted standards. His suggestions for reform are based on experience in one or more states.

It is foolish to expect that laws or rules regulating legislative ethics will have an immediate and obvious effect. Radical reform, which demands substantially more of legislators than they are willing to give, probably will produce evasion and cynicism. There is no advantage whatsoever to this. Moderate reform, of the kind advocated by Sacks, requires time until its effects take hold. Ethical codes and rules transform the environments of legislatures—not overnight, but gradually—and as new members enter, they are subjected to new and more demanding expectations, instead of old ones that condoned quite different behavior. For a while, it may be discomforting to individuals and legislative institutions. But even in the short term, the benefits of new standards are worthwhile, if not absolutely necessary. As Sacks writes, rigid adherence to the status quo is dangerous, because "public confidence in legislator integrity is often so low that action is required if the legislature is to maintain its proper place in our tripartite scheme of government."

III

If the legislature is really to become effective, lawmakers need opportunities to make significant contributions in productive political institutions. At its best, legislative life, with its uncertainty, ambiguity, and inconclusiveness, can be extremely frustrating. In most places, no one ever prevails, or not for very long. Usually frustration is even greater than can reasonably be expected, because many members have little chance to participate or to have real impact on legislative outcomes. This can be seen by considering for a moment standing committees and membership assignments. With few exceptions, work is unevenly distributed among committees in state legislatures, and opportunities to work in committee are unevenly distributed among members. When members, and particularly newcomers, are judged to have little to offer and are assigned to committees that have little to do, they can be expected to lose interest. As a result, the skills of many men are not being used, and this is detrimental both to the morale of individual legislators and the effectiveness of the entire legislature. Thus, a lack of institutional opportunities discourages members, who otherwise might have considerable potential; frustrated members, in turn, either leave the legislature completely or accustom themselves to the routine but not the productivity of service.

One of the most frequent recommendations to enhance opportunities for individual members and increase the effectiveness of the legislature is to create or augment professional staff. On the subject of staffing, there is virtual unanimity among reformers and substantial consensus among practitioners. Staff will provide the information necessary for the legislature to do its job. Arthur Bolton, formerly the director of the Office of Research of the

California Assembly and now a private consultant, makes a persuasive case demonstrating the advantages derived from capable staff. His essay is designed to illustrate a few proven methods of broadening legislative power to generate better answers to difficult problems. In it he describes staffing in California, and especially the role of the office of research, which was created only a few years ago by the California Assembly. Bolton details his office's activities and their impact with regard to smog and auto emission control, mental retardation programs, and chronic minority group unemployment in ghetto areas, showing that research conducted by the legislature can have significant impact. Because they are conducted by a body with the power and ability to act on the basis of knowledge, studies by the staff serve as a central forum for examining, debating, and solving major problems.

Bolton discusses a specific staff in a particular state. In my own essay in Part One, I explore some general questions with regard to professional staffing. Based on research on the impact of the creation of fiscal and caucus staffs in Wisconsin, I concluded that different types of staff have different effects on different individuals and groups in the legislature. One important point is that aides for members strengthen the rank-and-file, and thereby promote an individualistic power distribution; subject-matter staffs serving standing committees strengthen committee systems, and consequently promote a decentralized power distribution; and partisan staffs working for leaders or caucuses strengthen party agencies, and as a result increase centralization of power within the legislature. An effective legislature, in my opinion, depends on an internal balance of power; staff is one means by which an unequal balance can be redressed.

Staffing a legislature is no simple matter. First, there is the problem of recruiting and training able assistants. As Bolton writes: "It takes careful effort to develop a professional staff that understands the intricacies of the legislative process and combines subject-matter skills and political sensitivity." Some of the best staffers, quite like the best legislators, move on after brief periods of service. Second, there is the problem that legislators themselves have in coping with the assistance offered by staff. Bolton notes that "it takes time for legislators to learn how to use staff effectively." Some never learn, and some misconceive one very important consequence of staffing. The fact is that staff does not reduce the workload of individual legislators, as many would hope; rather, able and diligent staff discovers problems, suggests alternatives, complicates the legislative agenda, and thus creates more work instead of less for members.

IV

Staff can be extremely helpful, but it is no panacea. It will not make a poor legislature good nor a weak one strong. But it may make a poor legislature better, a weak one stronger. The same is true for other reform prescriptions. They undoubtedly help, and it is encouraging that during the past decade many states have adopted one or several of the reforms previously mentioned.

Take sessions, for example. In 1960 only nineteen state legislatures met annually, and nine of these were limited to budgetary matters during the even-year session. By 1970, as many as twenty-six legislatures were on annual sessions; only five of these were limited to budgetary questions in alternating years; and a number of others had the power to meet, by one means or another, in off-year periods.

Progress has also been made in the reduction of the number of standing committees in legislative bodies. Ten years ago, the average number of committees in houses was twenty-eight and in senates, twenty-three; by 1970, the averages were twenty-one and eighteen, respectively. During the decade, thirty-five houses and thirty-four senates cut down the number of standing committees; during the same period only six houses and seven senates increased the number, and then only slightly.

Legislator compensation has risen dramatically. In 1960, the median compensation for members was only $3900; ten years later, the median was $10,500, nearly triple the earlier figure. Almost every state has increased the salary for legislators, and in 1968–69 alone, as many as thirty-seven legislatures raised members' salaries. Legislative facilities have improved too. During the 1960s new office buildings or chambers were constructed in fourteen states. Staff services have also expanded. The decade saw the creation of sixty-seven service agencies throughout the state legislatures of the nation. The numbers of professional staff increased substantially. New and necessary emphasis was devoted to budgetary and fiscal affairs. Fourteen legislatures began to provide staff for the continuous study of state revenues and expenditures; fifteen established staff to review and analyze state budgets; and eleven created legislative postaudit agencies.

V

Progress has been notable. But legislatures still face severe challenges. Given the severity of the challenges, there is no assurance that representative assemblies will survive as more than vestiges of a dim past. William J. Keefe, whose essay appears in Part Three, is uncertain about the efficacy of reforms that have been proposed. "No one really knows," he writes, "whether major changes in the state legislative process, in structure or procedure, will make the legislature a better place in which to work, a more nearly equal partner to the governor, a more resourceful institution for the generation of innovative political ideas." Even with institutional reform, prospects are gloomy, Larry Margolis admits. "Whether the legislature can be saved," in Duane Lockard's opinion, "is . . . an open question."

The final essay in Part One of the volume is by Jess Unruh,

who served for almost eight years as speaker and then briefly as minority leader in the California Assembly. Unruh questions the efficacy of reform, although he more than anyone else was responsible for the giant strides forward taken by his legislature, and particularly the Assembly, during the past decade. Today, the California legislature measures up to practically all the standards set by reformers. It meets annually, in long sessions; its facilities are excellent; standing committees work rather effectively, not only in regular sessions but during interim periods as well; staffers proliferate, with some assigned to individual members, committees, caucuses, and leaders, and others working for central research bureaus or fiscal agencies; and only 120 members serve, each in a prestigious position, with salary and related benefits unequaled by legislatures throughout the nation.

Yet, Unruh is critical, believing that the California legislature is not working well the way it is now. (If this is the case in California, it would seem that no other legislative body is working very well either.) For him the most hopeful remedy would be unicameralism—one house instead of two. The only state with a unicameral legislature today is Nebraska, but the experience there provides little persuasive evidence one way or the other. It is impossible to attribute either the legislature's strength vis-à-vis the governor on the one hand or its lack of internal leadership on the other to unicameralism. How the legislature performs in Nebraska probably has more to do with the system of nonpartisanship, the small membership in the senate, and the political traditions of the state.

Unruh is convinced that unicameralism is necessary, since everything that is wrong with the legislature is doubled by having two houses. In his view, to continue tinkering with a bicameral system is tantamount to doing nothing at all. His arguments for the adoption of unicameralism in California and elsewhere are compelling. First, the checks and balances that operate between houses can often be disastrous, since they promote logrolling, log-jamming, and buck-passing, and make it exceedingly tough to enact progressive legislation. Second, unicameralism would result in considerable savings of both public and private funds. In California, Unruh estimates, the amount would be about twenty million dollars annually—in terms of legislator salaries, administrative time, and lobbyist expenses that are passed on to the public. Third, the single most important stroke to give the legislature greater visibility would be the move to unicameralism. More than anything else, this might restore public confidence in the state legislature.

Today unicameralism is not out of the question. It commands some support within legislatures and increasingly widespread favor outside. It is easy to conceive of successful constitutional initiative campaigns to create unicameral legislatures as a means of saving money and increasing efficiency. It would be a cruel irony if unicameral plans were adopted, not with the purpose of strengthening legislatures, but rather with the intention of reducing government and punishing politicians.

I believe that the picture is much more hopeful. The types of institutional changes that have been mentioned—ones that have been on the agenda for decades—are not the final word. No single one will make much of a difference at all. But taken together and skillfully implemented, they will create conditions under which legislatures—if leaders and members are so inclined —can become effective and fulfill important roles in the political, economic, and social lives of their states.

The Legislature as a Personal Career

DUANE LOCKARD

The object of this paper is to assess some of the reasons why the state legislature as a personal career has attracted too few able men and women, and to suggest some possible changes in legislative life that might remedy this crisis. For a crisis it is. The state legislature has declined in relative importance to an alarming degree within the past generation, and there is little on the horizon now to suggest that a renaissance is near. The decline of the American state legislature is admittedly not unique; legislatures the world over are in gradual eclipse owing to many contemporary developments. One hardly need stress the rising importance of the chief executive, the judiciary, and the bureaucracy. The conditions of our technological age dictate new roles for the technical expert, for the politically conspicuous chief executive in an age of mass communications, and, at least in the United States, for the judge in our tradition of the "political" judiciary. Big government, complex government tends to reduce the potential role of the legislature because it cannot avoid delegating authority and cannot retain the center-stage position of the highly visible governor.

Although the functions of the legislature have actually expanded in the past fifty years, its relative capacity for initiative, for creativity, and for authoritative control over government has diminished. Its once near total control over state finances is virtually gone in some states, and severely curbed in all. Instead of being a prime source of policy initiative, it now accepts or vetoes the initiatives of others. American state legislatures may put their *imprimatur* on more than one hundred billion dollars of public spending per biennium, but their discretionary control over those sums is far less than the detached observer realizes. Much public policy, being handled by the subordinate bureaucracy, is for all practical purposes beyond the control of legislators.

But more than these cosmic forces of technology and complexity are involved in the fading power of the legislature. Some of the decline is attributable to the shoddy behavior of some legislators, to the inept management of legislative business, and to the resulting poor image the public has of the legislator.

SAVING THE LEGISLATURE

Whether the legislature can be saved is in my opinion an open question. It would be tragic if its role were reduced still further. Perhaps because I was once a legislator myself—but not solely so—I conceive of the legislative body as an indispensable element of democratic government, providing, as it does, far more than is usually assumed to be its only role: the making of laws. It is vitally important as an agency that reflects the views of different elements of the state, that allocates resources between the private and public sector and also within government, that provides some kind of overview of the bureaucracy, and that mediates conflicts between competing forces.

Whether the legislature will be strong enough to continue to perform these functions depends in no small measure upon whether capable candidates will seek places in the legislative halls and stay there long enough to make a contribution. Although this sounds suspiciously like the old cliché that all we need is "better men" to solve a governmental problem, I have something a bit more significant in mind. The argument is this. Unless capable legislators opt for a legislative career, there will be no saving of the institution, for the very simple reason that there is no one else to do the job. The public is not interested. One must applaud the recent allocation of more than two million dollars in foundation funds to the study of the legislature, but the most that can be hoped for from this is the enlightenment of a few community leaders who may assist legislators in doing the salvage job. The community leaders can, for example, help get referenda accepted—admittedly a vital role—but the initiative can never come from them. Nor will the initiative come from the executive. As a matter of fact, we will be fortunate if the executive in many states will stay neutral, for the common attitude of some governors and many governors' staff men who work with legislators is that the last thing they wish to see is a more effective legislature—if by "effective" is meant anything but a body compliant to the call of the governor.

Renewed efforts at the recruitment of able legislators will also be inadequate. In the first place, our tools for effective recruitment are inadequate to the task. Although from time to time party leaders in a competitive situation will search out attractive candidates in order to win a seat, simple neglect of recruitment by the party is more common. Some party recruitment produces the opposite of ability. In eagerness to fill candidacies the wholly inept are at times tapped, or in search of compliant behavior, hacks are nominated. Self-recruitment is also common but hardly uniformly dependable. Recruitment by interests is equally bad or worse, for obvious reasons.

Thus the problem is to retain able legislators once they have entered the chamber by any route. James David Barber in his book, *The Lawmakers*, sets forth the qualities I have in mind. His ideal legislator is a man with technical skills to offer but even more importantly with a personality capable of a sustained and balanced performance. Barber stresses the need for self-confidence, a deep interest in public problems, ambition, a capacity to communicate and collaborate with others, and a considerable degree of personal security. One who has these attributes can withstand the heat of the political kitchen, but he may not feel that under existing circumstances the legislature is the place where his most significant contribution to the public weal can be made. Probably each of us could cite a sizable list of former colleagues who have these qualities but who abandoned a legislative career. Why do they leave when they might have offered so much?

WHY DO THEY LEAVE?

The reasons are numerous, and in the ensuing comments several sources of discontent will be cited. In each case single factors are an inadequate explanation for departure; the causes of discontent are interrelated, and the correction of any one of them—or the relative absence of them in a given state— does not stay the exodus. And in some states the tenure remains high despite the presence of the negative factors, although it may be the less competent rather than the able who persist.

Inadequate Salary

The median salary of state legislators, including their expense accounts in states where such exist, is quite low. And in the eight states that have the highest salaries the range has been from $7000 to $12,500. If the duration of the legislative session were brief, and if there were not heavy demands on legislators' time between sessions, at least the higher-paying states might seem to offer adequate compensation. But increasingly sessions are extended, outside duties multiply, and if a member is to take his job seriously he must spend an enormous amount of time keeping informed and rendering services that the constituency has a right to demand. In short, handling the scope of legislative duties adequately today is not a part-time but a full-time job. Only if a legislator has a profession that permits him to absent himself for long periods can he afford to take a legislative career seriously.

Admittedly the raising of legislative salaries to a full-time professional level would not necessarily result in a full assembly of competent members. The drones and hacks like a good income as well as the competent. But at least the competent *who would be able to earn a decent salary otherwise* would not be so likely to forfeit a legislative career if a minimally adequate salary were provided. It should be noted too that the effective conduct of legislative business is not going to be done in a sixty-day session; only if the sessions are extended will there be time to give adequate consideration to difficult problems, and it follows therefore that in the smaller and poorer states just as in the richer and larger ones much higher salaries are imperative to the retention of capable legislators.

Inadequate Facilities

One thing that discourages the serious legislator is the utter lack in nearly all states of adequate facilities for the individual member. Lacking an office for conducting business, he either falls into the habit of neglecting his duties or of attempting to do his job under highly frustrating conditions. Research assistance is normally unavailable, and even the provision of minimal clerical aid is lacking more often than not. A member representing a large constituency may be willing to handle his correspondence responsibly but be utterly unable to do so. Since legislators are harried and hurried generalists dealing with a broad range of special problems, they need aid in researching the issues they face, but if the facilities are absent, a member has one of two alternatives: try to do it all himself or neglect the digging that would make his efforts fruitful. Either way the competent are likely to be discouraged.

Clumsy Methods

An intelligent and ambitious man who wants to do his job well is likely to be sickened by the clumsy and grossly inefficient methods he faces in the legislature. Bills are lost (both intentionally and unintentionally); calendars get jammed so that decisions must at times be made on dozens—even hundreds—of bills within a single day. As the numbers of bills mount to the thousands per session, it sometimes becomes difficult—in the short run, impossible—to ascertain the status of a given piece of legislation. This is especially so during the crush at the end of session. Decisions are deferred on so many bills that confusion reigns during the last days of the session, practically forcing blind decisions. Committees do not operate in most states as serious agencies for the analysis of issues but as sifting devices at best, and the member must therefore rely on a hurried few minutes of explanation of bills—if that—as a basis for making up his mind. All this is calculated to minimize the opportunities for the exercise of rational judgment, surely a way of convincing an able legislator that there are better ways of contributing his services to society.

Conflict of Interest

The amateurism of some legislators is an inducement to conflict of interest. The part-time member does not feel himself to be more a legislator than a contractor, lawyer, teacher, or real estate man for the very obvious reason that he is a legislator

only marginally. The appearance of a lawyer-legislator for a
client before an agency over whose members he has at least
some control is ethically dubious at best. The real estate man
in the legislature making every effort to support his business
interest, while others fight for their special occupational interest,
is not calculated to raise the moral tone of nor the public
respect for the legislature. It would be fatuous to expect that
all legislators will cast aside and forget their special interests
once they enter the legislative arena—legislators are not judges,
and indeed should not be removed from active involvement the
way we expect a judge to be. But under present conditions
the short-term legislator is almost invited to maximize on his
legislative position for tomorrow's personal profit, if not today's.
If the legislative position is made more attractive and more
professionalism results, it may be possible to enact and enforce
more adequate regulations against conflict of interest. To be
sure, some of the most adroit practitioners of conflict-of-interest
manipulations are long-term members, and the reduction of
amateurism will not affect them in the least. The hope is, however, that more professionalism and higher standards of legislative
conduct will result from the changes here suggested and that
these in turn will make it possible to control flagrant cases of
conflict of interest.

Opportunities for Legislative Creativity

Some of the factors that limit the opportunity for creative
work by legislators are probably beyond recall. The limitations
on legislative activity that are welded into our constitutions
can be changed, if at all, only in the very long run. But at
the very least, legislators should resist the addition of such restraints as ear-marked taxes and specific prohibitions of actions that
on their own merits are not harmful. There are, however, other
restraints on creativity that are within the reach of the legislature,
and some of them have already been mentioned. For example,

the creativity of a legislator will surely be enhanced if he has the time, the facilities, and the staff with which to find out facts and apply his talents to them. The hurried and frantic pace of the last half of a typical legislative session is almost bound to discourage the capable legislator who wishes to make a substantive policy contribution but who is barred from doing so by the atmosphere of confusion.

CAN THE COMPETENT BE PERSUADED TO STAY?

There does not seem to me to be much doubt that many more able legislators might be persuaded to remain than is now the case if something like the following series of steps were to be taken. In the first place many able men already are able to stick it out, and if procedures and conditions are greatly improved the resulting milieu should prove particularly attractive to the types who can make a responsible and effective contribution.

Salaries and Facilities

As pointed out previously, considerably higher salaries would make it possible to increase the degree of professionalism in the legislature. If it is argued that higher salaries would prove equally attractive to the hacks of the political world, one can only admit the truth of the observation. However, under present conditions the odds in many constituencies would favor the competent over the hack. In the post-World War II era particularly, one can observe the stress that has been put on the recruitment of candidates with qualities attractive to professional and white-collar populations that have grown so rapidly in comparison with other groups. To be sure, there are districts where the party leadership does not have to put up such candidates and indeed seeks almost the opposite, but if there are any lessons to be drawn from the political developments of the past two decades, one of them is that it is increasingly risky to offer the public a hack.

Nor is there reason to fear that really attractive salaries might result in a permanent and unchanging membership. New members who are willing to exclaim publicly that the emperor lacks clothes are valuable, but newcomers would not disappear under a higher salary scale. The normal processes of attrition—death, defeat, retirement, ambition for other offices—ought to keep new personnel coming.

Annual and Longer Sessions

If professionalism is to be nourished, there is no alternative to lengthening sessions and making them annual. One of the most discouraging aspects of current practices is the hurried confusion of brief legislative sessions. Moreover, the brevity of legislative sessions becomes a rationalization for holding down legislative salaries, and indeed there is a problem in selling the public on the notion that high salaries are needed for what seems to them to be a few months of work every two years. To make the job equal to the salary is obviously necessary.

Putting Order into Legislative Operations

Legislators often complain about the inefficiencies of the bureaucracy, but even measured by the standards of public administration the legislature has to rank as one of the sloppiest operations in government. Probably this is accounted for in good part by the amateurism in the legislature and by the intermittent manner in which the legislature works, but whatever the reason, there is an enormous amount that could be done to improve legislative operations. Although comparing legislatures with business corporations may be dubious, it appears that the legislature operates like a country store at a time when the sophisticated methods of General Motors are available.

There are obvious improvements that could be made that would cost little and give beneficial results, and others that are not so obvious but that might also pay off. For example, a much more effective use of the present expenditures for staff is possible. In many states, perhaps most, there are more door-keepers and messengers than there is any use for. In the Connecticut Senate we happened, by no coincidence whatever, to hire exactly the same number of messengers and doorkeepers as there were members of the majority party, splitting the patronage one-apiece. A good many of those messengers—all of whom received the same pay then as did the legislators—failed to show up with any regularity, and in some cases the senators had to deliver the messengers' paychecks to them. Too many legislative councils and legislative committees are staffed by hacks who should be replaced with competent staffers. Likewise the clerical staffs of many legislative bodies are untrained and inefficient personnel whose main recommendation for being employed was their patronage claim.

If the legislature is to do its job in the appropriations field, for example, it must equip itself with a large and highly expert staff to at least compete with, though not necessarily match, the expertise on the other side of the fence. But the appropriations committee is not the only one needing assistance; the other important committees also need help. Indeed, only when the state legislature's committees begin to approach the level of serious work done in congressional committees will the legislature begin to do its job properly. The hearings, reports, and analyses that come from congressional committees are in good measure the result of having acquired and retained for long periods an able and loyal staff.

There are several possible uses of electronic devices that could also improve legislative operations. To begin with, all the larger chambers should install electronic voting machinery to speed up proceedings and simplify the tabulation of votes. It is possible also to program for a computer the whole of the state's body of statutes with a simple indexing system so that at any time either the staff or the legislator can find out immediately what aspects of existing law might be affected by a proposal. Thus a proposed change in the election law—often a highly complex body of statutes—could be more effectively evaluated if all the possible ramifications could be investigated quickly rather than depending upon the fallible memory of even a highly talented adviser. Of necessity there are aspects of the criminal law scattered throughout the statutes, and there are references to labor law, local government, and most other subjects outside the principal chapters devoted to those topics. Data retrieval devices would greatly facilitate the process of lawmaking simply by reducing the area of guesswork.

Electronic devices could also be used to keep tabs on the current status of legislation, especially in the larger states where the number of bills runs into the thousands. Simplified classification systems and orderly reporting methods from committees would keep the legislator fully informed on a day-to-day basis of the progress of all bills and proposals. No doubt ingenuity applied to the general problems of legislative procedure could produce many other comparable ways in which the legislature could borrow from the business corporation and the Defense Department in improving techniques.

In the last analysis the legislator is a generalist dealing with a wide array of specialists, in government and out. If a legislative career is to be attractive and if it is to be productive of sound policy output, then means must be found for specialization within the generalist's role. In my opinion the proposals suggested here and others that could be imagined, or that will develop from experiments attempted, would go a long way toward encouraging men to think of the legislature as a career. If that happens there is some reason to think that the legislature can save itself from further decline; if it does not, the future of the legislature at the state level is bleak indeed.

Revitalizing State Legislatures

LARRY MARGOLIS

In considering opportunities for and obstacles to legislative reform, we should first ask ourselves: Why revitalize state legislatures? Why not let them go? David Brinkley predicted that within the next twenty-five years the states are going to disappear anyway. Why have them? They are cumbersome and retarded. They don't do the job.

The uniqueness of the American experiment in democracy— the gamble that our founding fathers took—lies in a system that does not intend to be the most efficient, but one in which there is a possibility of achieving effective government while preserving the greatest possible degree of personal freedom.

To achieve both effective government and personal freedom, a rather complex system was devised that distributes power among units of government and among branches of government and pits them against one another. In the constitutional architecture that resulted, political power is distributed among the states and the central government and among the executive and legislative branches of the national government as well as the state governments.

If any of the elements in this intricately balanced and complex system is comparatively weak, the system does not work. In fact, it becomes dangerous. Imbalance in such a system can produce paralysis, because while there is a sufficient distribution of power to prevent action, there is not enough capability to perform and to respond to challenges.

THE NEED FOR REVITALIZATION

It has been said that to humanize government there needs to be cracks in the wall of the monolith of power of the state, so that people can dig in their fingernails and hang on. If we permit a development to occur in this country in which there is a concentration of resources and authority at one level of government and in one branch of government, there will probably be more efficiency but there will be no place you can dig in and defend yourself, no place to weather the storm of adverse governmental action.

Nevertheless, there is developing in this country today an impatience over the prospects of revitalizing the states and of strengthening state legislatures. This is evident in the emerging relationships between the cities and the federal government. It is also evident in the current trends in foundation grants. It can be seen in the business community's public affairs programs, which are almost exclusively directed to the "urban crisis." Such programs as the Urban Coalition, the Task Force on Economic Growth and Opportunity, the National Alliance of Businessmen, and the Urban Action Centers are only a few cases in point. They say, in effect, "Forget the states! They are not going to make it. The crisis is in the cities and we have to get at it there."

This reasoning contains a fatal flaw, and these efforts are not only doomed to disaster, they carry with them the added potential of destroying important elements of our political system. In the direct attack on the problems of the cities, it is possible to provide emergency relief—to put the finger in the

hole in the dike—but it is not possible, fundamentally, to recon-
struct the system so as to prevent the development of future
crises. Ultimately the funding and the authorization of programs
to rehabilitate the cities must come through the state legislatures.
If the state legislatures are not revitalized, we will never get
the fundamental reorganization that will avoid crisis—unless, of
course, we are prepared to abandon the state level of government
altogether. But there appears to be no real indication that we
are so prepared.

In a country as large, complex, and varied as the United
States there is an opportunity in the state system to experiment
with methods of dealing with problems. We have a number of
laboratories in the United States for experimentation. The types
of problems that we face today are such that no one has the
answers, and few even know the right questions to ask. But the
state system affords an opportunity to try various kinds of programs and attempted solutions. If they prove workable at the
state level, they can then be elevated to the national level.

The legislature is at the heart of the state governmental system.
The quality of state government is no better than that which
the legislature permits it to be. The legislature is the funnel or
the bottleneck through which the development of state government must flow.

THE MEANING OF REVITALIZATION

What do we mean by revitalizing legislatures? It means equipping them with the competence to meet problems of our society
at the level at which they arise and providing them with the
capacity to deal authoritatively with these problems, rather than
working in fits and starts and through last-minute crash programs
always too late to catch up with the crisis. In short, it means
enabling them to create the conditions for the good life. Neither
the state legislatures nor any other governmental instruments

can provide us with the good life, but they can provide the conditions in which we can choose among available options to construct whatever *we* regard as the good life.

Revitalizing state legislatures also means creating visibility for the legislature through which the citizenry can see what the legislature is doing and can react to what it is doing. A system must be constructed in which there is a very high political risk for the person who serves in the legislature, but coupled with that high risk is the opportunity to be effective and to get the job done. Such a system necessitates frequent referral to the voters, but provides ample authority to accomplish those things that compel the attention of the voters and cause them to be concerned about what their representatives are doing.

The legislature must be the arena in which major conflicts are resolved or mediated, and there must be an understanding on the part of the citizenry that the legislature *is* an arena. In an article in a national magazine about a year ago, a man who has covered the legislature in one of the states for many years said that if the legislatures would spend more time finding the *right* answers to problems instead of compromising among evils as much as they do, legislatures would not have such a poor image. The reporter should understand that the legislature is just the kind of arena in which there is no alternative except to choose among "evils," if you want to call them that, or "goods," if you prefer to call them that. "Evils" and "goods" are simply the same, looked at differently by different people. As the legislature engages in the process of resolving these conflicts or "choosing among the evils," the public witnesses a very disagreeable scene. Conflict is considered disagreeable. The public doesn't like or understand it and has a low regard for the arena in which it takes place. There is a strong preference for the cool, confident voice of the executive who resolves his conflicts in the privacy of his office and then announces in a firm, strong voice what his programs will be. Executive calm is reassuring, and legislative conflict is disconcerting.

A revitalized legislature is independent. It has independent sources of information on which to base its judgments, it has the independent capacity to innovate. If the governor chooses not to move on state problems, can we any longer afford to wait four years until there is a new governor? If the legislature is not equipped to produce and to originate—not simply to review the governor's proposals and to react to them—then the state will not respond when the problem arises. Continued lack of response will render the state irrelevant.

THE METHODS OF REVITALIZATION

What then must we do to revitalize state legislatures? How can we transform them into modern instruments of effective decision making? How do we overcome the drag they now exercise on state government? There must be a high degree of public awareness and concern about the legislature. But exhortation will not produce it. You cannot merely tell people that the legislature is important to them and they ought to interest themselves in it. We interest ourselves in things in which we must interest ourselves. If the legislature were more visible and had the capacity to affect significantly the quality of our lives, it would be unnecessary to exhort the public to pay attention to who gets elected to the legislature or how they act after they are elected.

Participation by the Public

Public awareness and concern result from participation. American assemblies, beginning with the Arden House American Assembly on the State Legislature and the subsequent regional and state assemblies that have now covered all the states, have helped to generate public concern about the condition of state legislatures in the United States. The program of the Citizens Conference on State Legislatures also contributes to this end. The Citizens Conference organizes and assists citizens commissions composed of the leading people of the state from all walks of life. These commissions work with the legislature in developing a program of modernization and improvement. When the people on these commissions take a look at the legislature, they become very concerned about the problem.

You cannot change the legislative system on a partisan basis. Too often the press is very happy to report the charges of one party that the other party is engaged in a raid on the public treasury when it suggests that the legislature spend the money that it takes to equip itself with the capacity to solve the states' problems. There are too many members of the legislature itself who see an opportunity, when someone else has marshaled the courage to take a stand for the institution, to "grandstand" at the expense of fellow members and at the expense of the legislature itself. A favorite ploy of some members is to say "We should be happy to serve without pay," or "We don't need staff or offices, that's just a waste of the taxpayer's money!" That may serve to help re-elect the representative of an ignorant constituency, but it does not do much for the legislature as an institution or for our system of self-government.

Legislative revitalization requires the participation of the business community, and this is central to getting the job done. There are too many conservatives in the United States who insist that the best government is the least government, as though we still live in an agrarian society. Since they cannot get at the federal government, they vent their wrath at the state because they can get at it by withholding resources or denying authority. An increase in the federal income tax is not submitted to a plebiscite, but a local school bond issue goes down to defeat in retaliation. The result is to create more centralism. If the job is not being done at the state level, the people turn to the federal government for the assistance, and the problem becomes compounded.

Recently one of the major corporations in the United States

was confronted very directly with the necessity to decide what position to take on legislative improvement. On the same day it received two communications. One indicated there was a bill providing for annual sessions of the legislature in a particular state, and the question was whether to support or oppose this bill. In the same mail the same officer of the corporation received a letter from a senator in a neighboring state apologizing for a bill that had just passed and that worked a severe hardship on the economic interests of this company. The bill was introduced, enacted by both houses by unanimous vote, and signed by the governor in two days. This senator was very sorry the bill had passed; he explained that the members of the legislature were unaware of its contents. He complained about the short sessions and how bills go sailing through with no opportunity for members to read or understand them. He promised that his first act in the next session would be to introduce a bill repealing this act. But the next session is twenty months away. Little wonder the corporation involved supports annual sessions of the legislature.

Items on the Agenda

Anyone who looks at the legislature comes to the same conclusion about what needs to be done. Every study arrives at the same result. The purpose of studies is not so much to discover what is wrong with the legislature or what the legislature needs, but rather to carry public opinion along in support of the recommendations that will inevitably result.

Legislatures need space in which to do their work, to conduct their business in dignity. The members need better compensation. They need salaries that are higher than anything anyone has yet proposed, including the recommendation made by the Committee for Economic Development. The CED recommendation that the salaries of the legislature be no less than fifteen thousand dollars a year in the smaller states and thirty thousand dollars a year in the larger states just begins to scratch the surface of the problem; and compensation is not salary alone, but retirement programs for members of the legislature that are superior to those in private industry or in state government generally. When you elect a member of the state legislature you are, in fact, asking him to give the most productive years of his life to public service in a very high-risk business. If you do not want him to feather his own nest because he is concerned about how to pay for the education of his children after he is no longer in office, you have to compensate him. You can say that it was his choice to run, you did not ask him. But that will not solve the problem.

Legislators need staff and they need a variety of kinds of staff: technical staff to collect information, policy staff that should be political, but competent. There are ways to increase the possibility of staff competence, but the first essential is to provide the staffing.

Legislators need time in sessions, which are unrestricted as to frequency, length, and subject matter. The problem of the size of the legislative body is important, too. Pennsylvania recently missed a great opportunity to make a significant improvement in the legislative system during this last constitutional convention when the size of the house should have been cut in half. If the degree of representation that they have in the Pennsylvania house were replicated in California, for example, California would have a house of about four hundred members, instead of the present eighty. Large size adversely affects all the other considerations that have to do with improving the legislature. It adversely affects the visibility of the legislature and the ability of committees to operate efficiently and effectively. It operates against the probability of equipping the members of the legislature adequately. This does not mean to say that the state of Pennsylvania could not afford to properly equip 203 members of the House. It could afford to equip a thousand members of the House, but the probabilities are against equipping the 203 present members.

The odds would be improved if there were only one hundred members.

The committee system needs reorganization. There should be fewer committees, and their jurisdictions should be broadened. The number of assignments members have could then be reduced. Published rules of procedure and majority rule should govern in the committee. Legislatures also need a system of orderly calendar for the conduct of floor business.

Finally, legislatures need leadership to achieve revitalization and this is the most important element of all. You can provide the conditions for all of these improvements and not get them unless there is leadership in the legislature that is willing to use its authority to strengthen the institution. If every member of the legislature uses his position to maximize his own interest or to benefit the interests he represents, then you will see no improvement, whatever amount of money is spent or staff provided. There are limits to the capacity of system design. Ultimately legislative improvement will depend on how organization and resources are used and what kind of leadership emerges. All that can be done is to provide the conditions under which leadership can arise and be nurtured. This is important, because there are many legislatures in the United States that purposely prohibit the development of any continuing leadership at all. They rotate leaders, allowing each man to serve only one term as presiding officer. New Jersey is an example.

BENEFITS AND COSTS

What progress can be reported on efforts to strengthen legislatures that have been under way now for the past few years? The catalogue of specific details has been published by the Citizens Conference on State Legislatures. Certainly, there is movement. The states in which greatest improvements have been made in the legislative system are California, most definitely, and to a substantial degree, Illinois. The other states in which important recommendations have been made recently include Minnesota, Utah, Kentucky, and Idaho. There are commissions operating and in the process of formulating recommendations in Iowa, Oregon, West Virginia, and Montana. There are commissions about to begin or in the process of being organized in Georgia, Ohio, Connecticut, Virginia, and Pennsylvania.

What will it cost to revitalize state legislatures? There is no state in the United States that spends more than 1 percent of the state budget on the support, maintenance, and operation of the legislature. Most state governments are billion-dollar-a-year enterprises. The closest thing we have to a board of directors for that enterprise is the legislature. The state of Wyoming permits its legislature to meet only forty days every two years. And there is not a single employee in the legislature. I heard someone suggest that Wyoming cannot really afford self-government, and that the people there should contract for it from a neighboring state.

Aristotle called politics the master science. By politics I understand him to mean the official decision-making mechanism in the society. I think he called it the master science because it is the mechanism by which all other decisions become possible. Our private decisions, what we choose to do with that part of our time or our money which is left over for private disposition, become possible only with a system in which political decisions can be made.

What we spend on the decisional part of the governmental-political system in the United States is rather uncertain. We do spend six billion dollars a year on liquor and four billion dollars a year on tobacco. I use both liquor and tobacco, so I am not overly critical of others consuming these goods. Yet we do not spend anywhere near half of that on the entire official decision-making apparatus, from local government to the Presidency of the United States. We surely need to readjust our values.

Even with the progress that has been made recently, I am still not in a position to say that I think the states are going to survive. It is not my purpose to paint an overly gloomy picture; I simply do not know. The issue is not clear. Some progress has been made, but there has been some deterioration at the same time. There is an opportunity for the states to make it, but I am not confident that we are going to take advantage of that opportunity.

Ethical Standards
in the State Legislature

HOWARD R. SACKS

In discussing legislative ethics it is important to avoid both the
zeal of the impractical reformer and the complacency—sometimes
approaching defensiveness—of those who fear any action. I hope
to avoid both extremes. Unlike some reformers, I do not favor
drastic restrictions on the private economic activities of legislators,
and I think that public disclosure of private economic interests is a
device to be handled with care. On the other hand, public confidence in legislator integrity is often so low that action is required if the legislature is to maintain its proper place in our
tripartite scheme of government.

The overwhelming majority of legislators are honorable men,
trying hard to maintain high ethical standards in a most difficult
set of circumstances. But there are occasionally a few whose conduct leaves something to be desired. The result is that the public—
aided by the news media—often jumps to the conclusion that
our legislatures are cesspools of corruption. So it appears that we
must face up to the fact that action designed to improve ethical
standards may be required.

The dilemma in nearly all the states is the dilemma faced by the legislator himself: legislative service is part-time service, and the legislator must earn a substantial portion of his livelihood on the outside. He must have a job, or run a business, or have investments, or perform services for clients. The legislator himself, or an employer or client, will therefore have particular interests in what state government is doing. The hapless legislator may thus find himself in a position where he is tempted, persuaded, or coerced to ignore his official responsibilities in favor of some private economic interest. And, since the legislator cannot subsist on his official salary—which is often shockingly low, even for part-time service—he cannot escape from these problems by simply cutting himself loose from private economic relationships.

Unless and until we decide to make legislative service fulltime—and neither reason nor current trends makes a compelling case for this change—we are going to have to live with the dilemma. Accordingly, a piecemeal approach is necessary. I therefore propose to discuss the several ethical problems confronting the state legislator, making some suggestions for dealing with each. Most of the measures that will be suggested have been tried in one or more states, and thus we have some experience to go on.

In discussing the problems I will exclude from consideration lobbying and campaign financing. Both of these are very important, but I am not attempting to cover them here. Let me note in passing, however, that solving the problem of campaign financing is particularly important in dealing with legislators' conflicts of interest. The reason is that even the best controls on conflicts of interest can be evaded through the giving of campaign contributions to legislators.

FINANCIAL INTERESTS OF LEGISLATORS IN
STATE CONTRACTS

I begin by discussing the problem arising out of financial interests on the part of legislators in state contracts. If, for example, a member of the legislature has a substantial stock interest in a construction company that has a contract with the highway department, there may be a problem. The difficulty is that the legislator may be in a position to influence the highway department, and even if he is not, the public may view the transaction with suspicion. To avoid these dangers, some states have statutes forbidding legislators to have financial interests in state contracts. Other states permit such interests where the contract is awarded through competitive bidding. This latter device, I think, is less effective than a complete ban.

A troublesome situation arises where the interest of the legislator is indirect, such as the case where he is an employee of a company holding a state contract, or where he owns a company that sells goods to a company holding a state contract. Although ethical problems can arise, it is very difficult to devise controls that would not be so sweeping as to discourage honorable men from entering the legislature. Then, too, we should avoid controls which could seriously interfere with the state's procurement processes.

BRIBERY LAWS AND PROHIBITIONS ON REWARDS
FOR OFFICIAL ACTION

Everyone will agree that we should have strong laws against bribery of legislators. Although bribery is infrequent, every such case does enormous damage to public confidence in the legislature, and poses a threat to the integrity of the legislative process.

The important thing is to have not just a bribery statute but a well-drafted bribery statute. A good example of such a statute is contained in the Model Penal Code. Some may want to go further to reach not only the case where the legislator sells his vote (a corrupt transaction), but the case where the legislator takes money without agreeing to do anything in return but *knowing* of the corrupt motive of the other party. A model is offered in the Illinois statutes. I personally am not at all sure that it makes sense to go beyond the provision in the Model Penal Code.

Closely related to the bribe is the reward. For instance, an individual or a group that is pleased with what a legislator has done in his official capacity may decide to reward him by giving him opportunities for economic gain. Acceptance of such opportunities creates dangers. Accordingly, it is wise to prohibit rewards for official action, and the prohibition should extend to the giver as well as the receiver.

LOBBYING FOR COMPENSATION

There are grave dangers to legislator impartiality and to public confidence when a legislator takes money for lobbying in his own legislature. Such conduct does not violate bribery laws if a legislator acts in his private capacity. Take the case of lobbying by a legislator who is a lawyer. Although this kind of lobbying is not common, it occasionally occurs. Something should be done about it, and a flat ban on such lobbying seems desirable. The ban should also cover compensated bill-drafting and legislative counseling.

To be fully effective such a prohibition on lobbying should also cover partners and other close associates of legislators. However, such a broad restriction could make it difficult for some men to serve in the legislature. Some firms would probably put pressure on their lawyers to give up legislative service rather than

abandon profitable lobbying employment. The choice here between fully effective controls on conflicts of interest and the
avoidance of interference with recruitment into the legislature
arises frequently. In the case of lobbying by law firms, the problem is very difficult to solve. My own preference—and it arises
in part because I think that lawyers make good legislators—
is to avoid strict controls, in order to preserve the flow of lawyers
into the legislature.

Accordingly, I recommend only disclosure as a control device.
This would work as follows: Any legislator whose firm was engaged in lobbying would have to make a public statement of that
fact, and he would have to identify the particular bill. He would
not have to identify the particular client by name but only by
the client's general type of economic activity, such as "savings
and loan association." Disclosure of compensated lobbying by
one's partners would be of some help, because it would alert the
legislator's colleagues to the danger of bias on the part of the
particular legislator. Moreover, it would put pressure on that
legislator to avoid taking action on the bill that would be dictated
by his firm's interest in having a satisfied client.

SUPPLEMENTARY COMPENSATION FROM
PRIVATE SOURCES

Legislators should not have their official salaries supplemented
by private parties, although legislators should be allowed to accept
compensation for private employment. A related and more difficult
problem arises when the legislator is provided with a fund for
official expenses, with the money supplied by private contributors. Funds of this kind at the national level have created a
very poor impression. The problem is what to do about them.
The best solution is for the legislature itself to provide its members with the kinds of services and facilities they need to perform
their important tasks. If this is not done, privately financed

expense funds may have to be allowed. Any legislator benefiting from such a fund, however, should be required to make public disclosure of the sources of the fund and the uses to which it is put.

LEGISLATOR INTERESTS IN LEGISLATIVE ISSUES

A very important and more pervasive problem is the conflict situation arising out of a legislator's personal interests in state legislation. A farmer is interested in farm legislation, a pharmacist may be interested in fair trade legislation, and a lawyer-legislator may have clients interested in a particular bill. These conflict situations—and I use the term "conflict situation" and even "conflict of interest" in a purely descriptive sense—are inevitable in a part-time legislature. I do not think we should try to eliminate all of them. The real question is what can be done about them.

The Divestment Device

The quickest and most effective device is to require legislators to give up their outside interests. There is some precedent for this. For instance, many states have laws or constitutional provisions forbidding dual office-holding. An official in the executive department is not allowed to sit in the legislature. Similar problems can arise where legislators hold public office at the local level. But little has been done about this. I am generally cool toward divestment (or severance) as a control device. Thus, I would be opposed to banning legislators from practicing law or requiring them to sell their stock in companies that have substantial legislative interests. It is questionable wisdom also to ban persons in selected occupations, such as schoolteachers, from sitting in the legislature. Such prohibitions do eliminate conflicts of interest, but they also eliminate expertise.

Nonetheless, divestment might be useful in carefully selected cases. For example, if state legislation on horse-racing had in a particular state acquired a bad aura, it might make sense to require legislators (and their families) either to get out of horse-racing or leave the legislature.

Another possibility would be to make leadership positions in legislatures full-time, i.e., prohibiting Senate Presidents and House Speakers and majority and minority leaders from engaging in outside employment. It would be surprising to find a governor practicing law on the side, especially if he had clients with vital interests in what state government was doing. Perhaps we should apply the same rule to legislative leaders—assuming that we paid them enough and made the prestige of their service sufficient, so that able men would not be discouraged from taking these important positions.

Codes of Ethics for Legislators

Bribery statutes do not reach far enough, and divestment is too strong a medicine to be used very often. As a result, a number of states have enacted codes of ethics for legislators. New York was one of the pioneers in this area, and California and Illinois have enacted comprehensive codes. Although it would be dangerous to claim too much for such codes, they do have a place in any scheme for controlling and eliminating conflicts of interest.

Any such code should be divided into two parts: one part on rules of conduct and the other on ethical principles. Rules of conduct are designed to be enforced by the legislature itself, using such sanctions as censure. In contrast, ethical principles are merely a set of ideals toward which legislators should aim and a set of standards designed to be helpful in dealing with conflict situations. No formal sanctions should be provided for violation of ethical principles. This structure for a code, incidentally, is similar to that found in the new Code of Professional Responsibility of the American Bar Association. Although it is not possible to discuss in detail the provisions that could be included in a code of ethics, I shall list some of them. A few, it should be noted, go beyond the problem of personal interests of legislators in legislative issues.

The first part of the code, the Rules of Conduct, which would be enforced by the legislature itself, could include:

1. A prohibition against acceptance of excessive gifts or hospitality from persons with legislative interests. There are some tricky drafting problems here. For example, we do not want to prohibit a legislator from accepting a Coke (or even a martini) from someone with legislative interests. Nor do we want to prohibit a legislator from accepting five thousand dollars in stock from his mother, just because she happens to have legislative interests. I am confident, however, that these problems can be solved and a meaningful provision devised.

2. Misuse of confidential information should be prohibited.

3. It may be desirable to include a general provision forbidding conduct "unbecoming a legislator." It is impossible to anticipate all the instances of improper conduct, and a catch-all provision—although capable of abuse by the enforcing authority—may be justified in an attempt to reach unpredictable abuses of trust.

The second part of the code, the Ethical Principles, should include provisions not meant to be enforceable by formal sanctions. These principles are designed to give the legislator a set of standards to help guide him through the awkward situations in which part-time legislators often find themselves. They are ethical principles rather than legal rules, because the provisions are either not specific enough or depend too much on a legislator's state of mind to permit enforcement by a government agency, including the legislature itself.

Some suggested provisions are:

1. Prohibit legislators from accepting excessive compensation or an excessive price in a transaction from a person with a legislative interest. An example would be a legislator engaged in public relations work who charges $1000 to a client with legislative interests, when the normal charge for the service would be only

$250. Such overcharging could be a thinly disguised bribe, and, in any event, it would look bad.

2. Insofar as feasible, given the fact that legislative service is part-time, legislators (and their close economic associates) should avoid accepting or retaining economic opportunities that present a substantial threat to their objectivity.

3. Where possible, a legislator should avoid accepting or retaining an economic opportunity that could create a reasonable suspicion of impropriety.

4. No legislator should accept or retain an economic opportunity if he knows that a major purpose of its offer was to influence or reward the legislator for his official discretion. This provision is suggested to deal with "influence" cases where some person or company with a legislative interest avoids a direct bribe to a legislator, but instead gives him a lucrative economic opportunity, such as a law case. Actions of this kind seem particularly reprehensible and can do great damage to public confidence in the integrity of the legislative branch. "Reward" cases are less serious, but also ought to be dealt with by an ethical provision.

5. No legislator should accept compensation arising from employments involving lobbying or drafting or counseling on legislative matters, when the service is performed by a professional colleague.

6. Optional disqualification in conflict situations should be encouraged. Mandatory disqualification of legislators is a device that has been little used in this country. I propose no change, since I think that compulsory abstention is a poor device for controlling conflicts. One reason, among others, is that compulsory abstention would probably knock out many more unbiased votes than "tainted" votes, i.e., votes actually affected by a conflict situation. On the other hand, voluntary disqualification often makes sense. Following are some suggested considerations to help the legislator decide when to participate or abstain:

a. Whether a substantial threat to his independence of judgment has been created by the conflict situation.

b. Whether his participation affects public confidence.

c. Whether his participation is likely to have a significant effect on the disposition of the matter. (If the bill is doomed to defeat or certain to be passed, what is gained by the legislator's participating in the decision?)

d. Whether the effective functioning of the legislature requires the legislator to participate.

e. Whether the legislator owes a duty to advise constituents of his position on the matter.

Abstention from participation may relate to any or all of a legislator's functions, such as voting, introducing or sponsoring legislation, attempting to influence decisions on any legislative matter, accepting or exercising a position of leadership within the legislature, and giving assistance in legislative drafting and counseling to persons who are also clients.

If a legislator disqualifies himself, he should disclose that fact. An optional disqualification standard should also make clear that a legislator need not abstain if he desires to participate in a manner contrary to the economic interest that creates the conflict situation.

7. When a legislator chooses to participate in a particular matter, despite the existence of a conflict situation, he should serve the public interest, and not the interest of any private group. To be sure, this states the obvious, but it may sometimes be helpful to have a clear statement of public duty for the benefit of those who may find it easy, or convenient, to have some doubts.

Ethical Principles for Interest Groups and Close Economic Associates of Legislators

It often takes two to create a conflict situation. In establishing rules, there is no reason to single out legislators and exempt those who help create or exploit these conflict situations. Accordingly, it may be desirable to have ethical principles established by the legislature for persons with legislative interests and for close economic associates of legislators, such as law partners.

Among the ethical principles that could be included are:

1. Persons and groups with legislative interests should abstain from improper attempts to obtain influence in the legislature. They should avoid conferring economic opportunities on legislators—such as sales of stock below fair value, legal cases, or insurance, realty, or other business—where a major motive is to affect a legislator's official conduct or to create good will toward an interest group. Those in positions of leadership in, or counsel to, persons or groups with legislative interests have a special responsibility to help restrain them from improper conduct of this kind.

2. Persons closely associated with a legislator in a partnership or other association should avoid accepting economic opportunities if there is a substantial possibility that these opportunities are being offered in an attempt to influence the legislator member of the partnership or association.

Although there would not be sanctions for violation of these ethical principles, it might make sense for a board of ethics to be established. Such a board (to be discussed below) would have the power to: investigate alleged violations; make findings of fact; communicate its findings to the legislature, bar associations, and similar groups; and recommend additional controls over those who create or exploit conflict situations. Though not very strong, these enforcement powers could sometimes lead to effective action; at a minimum, they would remind private interests and the general public that it often takes two to create ethical problems for legislators.

DISCLOSURE OF ECONOMIC INTERESTS BY LEGISLATORS

A particularly lively topic in any analysis of ethical problems of legislators is public disclosure of economic interests. Some states, such as Illinois, have such provisions. Certainly, disclosure is entitled to serious consideration in any jurisdiction where conflicts are a problem. The following are the *potential* benefits of disclosure, as they were set forth by the Illinois Conflict of Interest Laws Commission in its 1967 report:

1. By making public information on economic interests and relationships that can produce conflicts, disclosure would encourage legislators to be more careful in their extralegislative economic activities, and to deal with conflict situations in a way that would not expose them to charges of impropriety.

2. It would provide useful information to voters and other legislators, thus better equipping them to protect the public interest against the biased viewpoints that can result from involvement in conflict situations.

3. By making clear just what economic interests a legislator has, it would eliminate suspicion and rumors, thus protecting the innocent legislator against unfair allegations of conflict of interest.

4. It would facilitate enforcement of criminal provisions on conflicts, and of the rules of conduct contained in the Code of Conduct.

A sound disclosure plan should require periodic filings by legislators of the following types of economic interests:

1. A list of economic interests of the legislator and members of his immediate family (spouse and minor children residing with the legislator), whether in the form of stocks, bonds, realty, equity interests in proprietorships or partnerships, or otherwise. Exempted could be: (a) interests in the form of accounts in banks, credit unions, and savings and loan associations; and (b) in the case of equity interests, interests valued at less than five thousand dollars and representing less than 5 percent of the total equity interests in the entity.

2. A list of offices, directorships, and salaried employments of the legislator and members of his immediate family. Excluded, however, would be offices and directorships in political, religious, charitable, and educational groups, if the compensation were less than one thousand dollars per year.

3. A list of entities having substantial legislative interests, actual or probable, to whom the legislator was furnishing compensated services, such as clients receiving legal services. Services furnished by professional colleagues, such as law firm partners, would also be disclosed, if the legislator had knowledge of such activities. This provision would cover not only lawyer-legislators but insurance agents, real estate brokers, public relations specialists, and others furnishing services. Excluded from disclosure would be entities for whom the services furnished were valued at less than one thousand dollars during the period covered by the report.

4. A list of unsecured debts of the legislator and members of his immediate family, if any one debt, or the total thereof, exceeded a particular figure, say, five thousand dollars.

5. Other interests that could create serious conflicts, if so determined by the agency, such as a board of ethics, enforcing disclosure.

The agency would also be empowered to require disclosure of conflict situations as they arose (*ad hoc* or spot disclosure) if it determined that disclosure of interests was insufficient. However, it would be the unusual case where disclosure of interests would need to be supplemented by disclosure of particular conflict situations.

These provisions would not require the legislator to state the money value of any particular interest, or, except in rare instances, the name of the company in which he had an economic interest. Thus, disclosures like the following would be permissible: "employed by a school district"; "director of an auto casualty insurance company"; "stock in an apartment house"; "a client who operates an auto sales agency"; "officer of a labor union." If the entity were a registered lobbyist, it would have to be identified by name. The agency, moreover, could require more specific disclosure, asking, for example, that the description "manufacturing company" be amplified by an indication of the principal product or products of the company.

Candidates for the legislature, as well as sitting legislators, should be covered by disclosure rules. Disclosure statements would be kept up to date by periodic filings, and the information disclosed would be open to the public. Criminal sanctions should be provided for failure to file or for false filings.

Having outlined the potential benefits of disclosure and the elements of a disclosure plan, it is necessary to examine the case *against* disclosure. Listed below are some of the usual arguments made against disclosure, together with evaluative comments.

1. Disclosure might result in excessive attention being given to *motives* for legislator action at the expense of consideration of the *merits* of legislative issues.

2. Disclosure might result in unnecessary abstentions. A perfectly honorable man might disqualify himself, even though he was certain that he could cast an honest vote, if he knew that the conflict situation would become public. This is a danger. In the long run we must hope for more informed press coverage of conflict situations and a more sophisticated electorate, so that conscientious legislators would be less fearful of performing their official duties when confronted by a conflict situation. In the short run, it is probably true that there would be some cases where the public would needlessly lose the services of an honorable legislator.

3. Disclosure might unjustifiably invade the privacy of legislators and others with whom they had economic associations. Clearly it does invade privacy. However, legislators tend to live in something of a goldfish bowl now.

4. Disclosure might hamper recruitment of capable people into the legislature. For instance, disclosure of legal clients would sometimes lead to charges of impropriety. Clients do not like such publicity and neither do senior partners of law firms. Would disclosure tend to chill the interest of lawyers in legislative service? No one knows the answer. The author's limited study of this matter leads him to conclude that the costs in terms of lawyer recruitment are likely to be small.

5. Disclosure might lead to false charges of improper conduct, since the information could be distorted by the irresponsible or the malicious. The risk is certainly there, especially since we are operating in a political context. Some things can be done to reduce the risks. For instance, provision could be made for advisory opinions so that a legislator could obtain the advice of an official group before establishing or maintaining an economic relationship that might call his conduct into question. Moreover, a quite limited study by the author of what happened to some lawyer-legislators involved in public controversy over conflicts of interest indicated that it is the rare case where an innocent legislator is damaged by a false charge of misconduct.

6. Disclosure might violate the lawyer-client privilege. The author's research into this issue leads him to conclude that in the vast majority of cases disclosure would not violate the privilege. In any event, the legislature could limit such a privilege, assuming that it has no constitutional foundation.

7. A major question about disclosure is whether it would increase or decrease public confidence in legislator integrity. It has been argued that it would increase confidence, because it would show that the extent of the problems has been exaggerated. Assemblyman Smith's colleagues may suspect that his enthusiasm for branch banking may have something to do with a client interest, but they cannot be sure. Given disclosure, if no banks showed on his list of clients, such suspicions would tend to vanish. But there is another side to the coin. Although the public may be skeptical about the integrity of legislators, their understanding of conflicts of interest is more a matter of feeling than fact. Given disclosure, they would get facts. It is easy to imagine headlines like these: "Five Lawyer Members of State Senate Admit Clients Interested in Tax Bill" or "Assembly Majority Leader Discloses Legal Work for Oil and Gas Interests." It is hard to defend a negative—to argue that a vote on a particular issue was not influenced by a client, but rather by ideology or political factors. At least in the

short run, disclosure could make the public even more suspicious and cynical about the integrity of lawyer-legislators.

But the novelty of disclosure may wear off. One has the impression that reports of campaign contributions and lobbying expenditures often receive little public attention, perhaps because people have become accustomed or inured to the facts revealed. The same thing may happen to *ad hoc* disclosure and client disclosure—in the long run at least.

It is likely to be less damaging to the public confidence (and to the legislator's own reputation) if the legislator himself discloses information regarding a conflict than if it is revealed at some later point by a newspaper or a political opponent. Disclosure may in fact help to persuade the public that the legislature wants to control conflicts of interest. And a refusal to establish disclosure provisions may create suspicion that legislators have something to hide.

My own judgment is that arguments against disclosure do not add up to very much, but it would take a field study of a comprehensive disclosure plan, such as that in Illinois, to provide us with a more solidly based judgment. But would disclosure really achieve the benefits outlined at the beginning of this discussion, such as discouraging legislators from involving themselves in questionable economic relationships and making them more careful in how they deal with conflict situations? A study of the New York disclosure statute, conducted by the Illinois Conflict of Interest Laws Commission in the mid-1960s, showed that the New York statute had not produced significant benefits. On the other hand, no one has studied the effects of a more comprehensive statute, such as that in Illinois. What we need is a thorough study of the Illinois experience. Pending such a study, my own view is that a comprehensive disclosure plan is well worth trying in any state where the private economic interests of legislators are believed to constitute a serious problem.

REPRESENTATION OF PRIVATE CLIENTS IN MATTERS
BEFORE STATE AGENCIES

Legislators often are requested by constituents to represent them in dealing with agencies in the executive department. This is traditional in the United States and generally serves a useful purpose. However, when legislators (almost always lawyers) take money for such representation, problems arise. The danger is that since the legislature has control over agency budgets, personnel, and powers, an agency may be tempted to give undue deference to a powerful legislator who is appearing on behalf of a private client. Even if an agency does not yield to this temptation, the appearance of impropriety can damage public confidence. Compensated representation of clients before state agencies can also lead to "influence peddling," whereby a lawyer-legislator tacitly or explicitly indicates that he can wield special influence over a particular department because of his position in the legislature.

This problem is often a serious one. Once again, however, we confront the dilemma: truly effective controls, such as a flat ban on compensated representation before state agencies, may drive good men out of the legislature. The nature of law practice today makes it very difficult for any lawyer to avoid some dealings with state agencies on behalf of his clients.

A few states, however, have limited compensated representation by lawyer-legislators. Perhaps the most drastic restrictions have been imposed by California, where control was coupled with a substantial increase in legislator compensation. Massachusetts has imposed more modest restrictions. To my knowledge, however, no one has examined these reform programs in terms of comparing the benefits gained with the losses, if any, to the legislature of capable lawyer members.

In a state where the problem does not appear serious or where there is reluctance to run the risk of a major or total prohibition of this practice, the following measures may achieve a modest amount of control over the problem:

1. Judicial review of agency action is certainly helpful. It provides a substantial safeguard against harm that can result from undue influence exerted by a legislator on behalf of a client. It should be made clear, incidentally, that such influence can arise even where the legislator himself does not attempt to exploit his position. The very fact that he is in a position to help or harm the agency before whom he is appearing can induce that agency to do things for him that it would not do for the ordinary lawyer.

2. It may also be helpful to have some provisions in the code of ethics on representation cases. In Part I, the Rules of Conduct section, the following provisions may be helpful. First, a legislator should not state or imply that he is able to influence improperly or upon irrelevant grounds any state agency or official. Second, a legislator should not use improper means to influence a state agency or official in a case in which he, or a close economic associate, is participating. In the Ethical Principles section of a legislator, such as a law firm partner, should not accept a representation cases. First, a legislator, or any close economic associate of a legislator, such as a law firm partner, should not accept a representation case where there is substantial reason to believe that it is being offered in an attempt to obtain this legislator's influence over a state agency. Second, a legislator should not accept a case unless he believes there is merit to the position he is being asked to represent. Third, a legislator retained in a representation case should arrange, wherever feasible, for another person, such as another member of his law firm, to make appearances before the particular agency. A word of explanation about these two last principles may be helpful. The first merely reaffirms provisions of the new American Bar Association Code of Professional Responsibility, which forbids lawyers to handle cases that they believe have no merit. The second is based on the theory that the

personal appearance of a legislator before a state official can be embarrassing, and that if such appearances can be minimized, the danger of distortion of official decisions would be decreased.

3. Also worth consideration is a law authorizing or directing the state attorney general to intervene in any proceeding before a state agency when he thinks that there is danger that a lawyer-legislator's representation of a private client might prejudice the public interest.

None of the above devices will eliminate all the dangers. Hence, some may believe it wise to ban representation in types of cases where the greatest dangers of undue influence exist, or where the appearances of evil might be quite serious. These areas are likely to vary from state to state.

ENFORCING THE RULES

Important to the maintenance of high ethical standards is effective enforcement of whatever rules are adopted. Some rules, such as the bribery laws, should be enforced through the normal criminal processes. The enforcement of an ethics code should be left to the legislature. The usual enforcement agency is an ethics board. Here we come to a very sensitive question: Should an ethics board be made up solely of legislators or should it also include public members? Legislatures traditionally are very reluctant to include outsiders on ethics boards. This reluctance is easy to understand. Nonetheless, I believe that the maintenance of public confidence in the objectivity of an ethics board and of a favorable public image of the legislature require that a board have a strong complement of public members.

Less controversial, but nonetheless important, are the functions and powers of an ethics board. I suggest the following as a minimum:

1. To inquire into complaints of violation of the Rules of

Conduct. Where violations are found the board should make a public report to the appropriate chamber of the legislature. Only that house should have power to administer sanctions, such as censure. The board itself should not be able to punish legislators. That task should, for both constitutional and policy reasons, remain with the legislature itself.

2. To give advisory opinions to legislators on ethical questions. This important power not only helps guide the perplexed legislator, it can also protect him against press or political criticism subsequent to the particular action about which he has ethical doubts.

3. To administer whatever disclosure provisions are adopted.

CONCLUSION

The approach I have taken lies along the line of legal and quasi-legal controls. Yet it is quite clear that other things can be done that will help maintain high ethical standards and public confidence in the integrity of the legislature.

Improving compensation for legislators may help draw better men into legislative service and help keep them there. It may also reduce the temptation to engage in questionable conduct. Better facilities and services, especially staff services, should make it easier for legislators to guard against the biases induced by their own economic interests and, for that matter, pressure brought by lobbyists. Greater respect by citizens for public officials would also be helpful. Private groups, such as bar associations and other occupational groups, can also help by setting high standards for their members. A vigilant press can also be an enormous help by exposing wrongdoing. But the press sometimes presents ethical problems in an unduly sensational manner. Newspapers and radio and television stations, when considering publicizing a conflict situation, should remember that men's reputations are involved. Finally, employers of bright and honest men and women who are interested in politics should go to great lengths to make it possible for them to serve in legislatures.

The most effective stimulus to ethics legislation is a good scandal. Accordingly, reformers should, in at least one sense, pray daily for sin. In framing laws or codes it makes no sense to single out the legislature itself or any group within the legislature, such as the lawyers. Any code of ethics should not focus on lawyer-legislators, but should cover all legislators. Ethics legislation should probably also cover other branches of government, perhaps even the judiciary. In some states it has proved helpful to have a commission, including public members, study these complicated questions and report to the legislature. Such commissions cannot only lend prestige to a set of recommendations but also can engage in careful study of what has been done in other states and how effective it has been.

I have tried to paint a realistic picture of the ethical problems facing the part-time legislator. I have suggested that, while radical reform may be unnecessary, rigid adherence to the status quo may be dangerous. Even in states that have escaped scandal there is no guarantee that tomorrow will be like today. In outlining a program I have tried to keep in mind the need for maintaining the flow of able men and women into the legislature and the need for avoiding measures that interfere substantially with the effectiveness of the legislature. The program will not produce the millennium, but it should maintain and even improve existing standards. As part of a much wider program for strengthening the legislative arm of state government, a legislative ethics plan has its rightful place.

Expanding the Power
of State Legislatures

ARTHUR BOLTON

A legislature provides an organized and representative way of exerting power to reshape the natural environment and the social climate. The proper purpose of a legislature is to enact policies that will maximize each citizen's opportunity to enjoy life; or help him cope more effectively with his personal misery; or at least prevent the establishment of policies that damage the natural and social conditions of living.

Legislators have the power to limit, by law, what individual citizens may and may not do. They can affect the distribution of wealth within a state. Their actions influence how young people will be educated, how the state's public service systems will be structured, and who will be served.

Although legislators have great power to make policy, too often this power is used only to formalize policies that have been developed outside the legislature. Most proposed legislation comes from special-interest groups or state bureaucracies. An increasing number of important policy choices are left to the federal government, and state legislation in these fields merely allows the state to conform to federal requirements.

The purposes of this paper are to clarify why the underutilization of state legislative power often results in costly mistakes and to illustrate a few proven methods of broadening legislative power to generate better answers to difficult problems.

THE LIMITS OF ADMINISTRATIVE SPECIALISTS

As public problems have become more complex, many state legislatures have increasingly depended on the administrative branch of government, with its numerous experts, to provide the answers and suggest the policies of the future. If legislatures relinquish initiative to the "experts" in state or federal bureaucracies, they invite the erosion of their leadership and public apathy toward their activities. They may also fail to solve the problems of the state.

There are several reasons why the administrative branch of government, no matter how well-intentioned, is handicapped in designing imaginative alternatives. First, unlike the bipartisan legislature, the administration is much more partisan—much more likely to screen out proposals that depart from the ideology of the party in power. Thus a good idea may never reach the legislature for review because of partisan political considerations.

Second, complexity has forced an arbitrary and counterproductive fragmentation and specialization of knowledge. The advice of the "expert" should always be questioned, for he often has partial vision and tends to see issues from his own vantage point. Most of the state agencies relied on by governors for policy alternatives are directed by specialists with a single professional viewpoint (the department of highways by engineers, the department of health by doctors, the department of social welfare by social workers). These specialists, tightly organized in their own separate departments of government, find it almost impossible to initiate a multidisciplinary response to a problem.

This is not surprising, since quite often the professionals have very different and conflicting theories about the causes of a problem and the goals of state policy. For example, the people in the department of natural resources, who are concerned with recreational facilities and the preservation of scenic beauty, may conflict with the people in the department of highways, who are primarily concerned about the most economic movement of bodies and freight. The psychiatrists in the mental health department may favor a medically directed solution to the problems of delinquency, whereas the experts in law enforcement may push for more police, while the educators proclaim answers in improved reading programs, and the social workers stress family counseling. Are they all correct? Is one more right than the others? Or is it possible that none has answers that really work?

The fact is that most state agencies have a narrow view of the problems they deal with and the range of available solutions. Functional agencies invariably have ideological, professional, and institutional interests that cramp their reactions and limit their imagination. Thus they propose "more of the same" rather than something different.

Yesterday's poorly designed program tends to become an entrenched force that must be pushed aside for each new answer. But, as is often the case with government, yesterday's answers persist for years in the countless layers of old bureaucracies that never die but sometimes fade away after retirement ends tenured careers. At times they expend great energy to protect civil service positions in old programs that have outlived their utility. Yet these are the same people governors use to develop the "new solutions" that are then presented to the legislators for hurried review and approval.

Further, most departments of government are not in a position to publicly propose needed changes in the activities of *other* departments whose actions impinge on their own. It is considered poor form for one agency to propose that another agency go out of business, transfer its functions, or change its style of work. But behind the scenes, the warfare between bureaucracies and the different professional disciplines that run them is often unbelievably bitter.

There is yet another reason why state agencies are not in a good position to analyze the status quo and propose change. Most change hurts and is resisted. Change may upset old relationships or challenge traditional behavior. But if change *is* needed, it is precisely because the old traditional ways are not working. And it may be necessary to expose the failures of existing programs in order to create a public awareness and a political climate for eliminating or changing the old programs and replacing them with new ones. *We cannot rely on an agency that is operating a program to expose its own inadequacies.* Agencies almost invariably defend their own programs and, like living organisms, protect their vulnerable parts.

Because of dependency on administrative initiative, legislators enact many poorly conceived government programs that fail. All our past mistakes linger to poison the present image of state government, and public disenchantment and cynicism about politicians and legislatures grow. The affluent complain about paying high taxes to support programs that show meager results, and the poor, the recipients of government services, lose faith in the whole system.

SOURCES OF INDEPENDENT INFORMATION

Where can legislators get independent information, and how can they design original legislation without having to rely on the administrative branch? One obvious resource is the legislative advocate, or lobbyist. He is usually ready, willing, and frequently very able to provide information and advice. But this "free" source of help is certain to supply information and alternatives favorable to the interests he is paid to represent. Legislators rarely have the time, and frequently lack the expertise, to balance the conflicting viewpoints provided by various special interest groups, and they may be unaware of important opinions not represented by any lobbyist.

There are ways to strengthen the independence of legislatures. There are ways to equip legislators so they can create their own proposals and do a better job of analyzing the bills that originate with the governor, the state bureaucracies, and other special-interest groups.

It is generally known that California has the best staffed legislature in the nation. For many years we have had about one hundred budget analysts, attorneys, and auditors serving both houses of the legislature. These technicians help legislators examine the governor's budget proposals, draft bills, and provide legislators with legal counsel and independent fiscal information.

Since 1961, when Jess Unruh assumed the speakership of the California State Assembly, the Assembly has further developed its staff services to expand the capability of individual legislators and legislative committees. Each assemblyman has a secretary and an administrative assistant in his district office to improve his communications with his constituents. Each of the twenty-two bipartisan policy committees in the Assembly has a committee secretary and at least one full-time professional consultant with good understanding of the committee's area of concern.

Committee consultants analyze bills for the members of the committee, help raise pertinent questions, check the factual reliability of data presented by proponents and opponents of legislation, and offer committee members suggestions for amending bills to improve them. In addition, committee consultants help policy committees in carrying out studies that frequently result in committee-sponsored bills. Committee consultants are selected for subject-matter skills and ability to work well with all the members of bipartisan committees. They are not political appointees. Most committee consultants have survived changes

of committee chairmen—even when the new chairman represents
a different political party than his predecessor.

In the mid-1960s the Assembly also provided a separate research
staff of nine researchers for the minority caucus to extend the
power of minority members to originate their own legislation.
The resulting competition in ideas has helped to raise the level
of partisan debate. Increasingly the battle between Democrats
and Republicans is over who has the better idea rather than
who has the votes. (In California, the legislature is now so
closely divided that bipartisan support is needed to pass most
major bills.) In addition to originating proposals for legislation,
the minority staff also assists its members to develop amendments
to majority-sponsored proposals, thus converting them into more
mutually acceptable bills. This is not to say that all is harmonious
and that partisan power is not a determining factor in many
instances. But the existence of a minority staff does provide
greater opportunities to develop compromises so that statesman-
ship can replace narrow partisanship.

THE CALIFORNIA ASSEMBLY OFFICE OF RESEARCH

Not long ago the California Assembly took another important
step by creating its own Office of Research to equip itself to
conduct extensive independent studies. The significance of the
office is that it provides a comprehensive look at state problems.
It is now generally accepted that among the toughest obstacles
to social progress are the countless agencies that have been
created over the years, each with its own territory to command,
each with its own professional bias and rigidity, and each incapable of coping with totalities because each deals with small
fragments of large problems. The legislature has intensified
this problem by maintaining *in its own structure* these same
separations. So we see social welfare, public health, budget, and

tax committees each looking at the same issue—medical care, for example—from a different vantage point.

In our new Assembly Office of Research we have a staff of sixteen professional people with no agency loyalties or dogmas to defend. We are now able to apply teams of experienced researchers to problems that cut across lines of committee responsibility or require more attention than the small committee staffs can give. Free from day-to-day routine of committee work, these teams can devote as long and as intensive an effort as a problem may require.

During its first year, the Office of Research, in addition to helping individual assemblymen on independent projects, had a major role in the creation and passage of the Mental Health Act of 1967, which revolutionized commitment procedures in California. We are now working on such fundamental problems as smog, unemployment, criminal deterrence, and gun control at the request of various committees.

Several projects recently conducted by the California State Assembly illustrate elements of effective legislative research.

The first requirement of a successful project is that it begins with a serious commitment to solve some problem. The questions that should be asked are: Is the problem sufficiently important to justify research activity? Is there sufficient interest and willingness on the part of enough legislators to *act* if the research indicates a need for action? Staff members must work closely with members of the legislature in formulating research projects so that the alternatives to be considered will be technically and politically feasible.

Estimating political feasibility is a special requirement of legislative research. The product of legislative research is not a study report or publication in a prestigious professional journal —but a bill that can pass both houses and be signed into law by the governor. Our research projects must explore the most politically acceptable alternatives at the time. There is an obvious danger to conducting effective research within political constraints. Just as it is a mistake to invest time, energy, and money in projects that are clearly politically unrealistic, we have learned to avoid the tendency to be intimidated by what *appears to be* the political climate. We are learning that legislative research can be bold. Legislation that may have been considered politically impossible prior to a research project may emerge as the only politically proper solution when the facts have been collected and made public.

This apparent contradiction between the need to function *within* the limits of the politically possible and the need to push *past* those boundaries for imaginative solutions produces a unique characteristic of legislative research. *The research itself can be used as a means of testing and changing the political climate.* The legislative research project may alter the phenomenon being studied at the very moment it is being studied.

Vehicle Emission Control Legislation

Our Assembly Transportation and Commerce Committee has just completed a careful study of the serious smog problem in California. During the course of this study the committee found that practically 90 percent of the problem in Los Angeles County and other major population centers comes from automobile exhaust; that our present vehicle emission control measures have limited value; that if further controls are not applied, smog will become far worse within the next decade; that smog is becoming a massive public health problem; that the technology exists to reduce the problem significantly within a short time; and that the primary obstacle to solving the problem is the powerful automobile industry, which at the time we began our research was pushing for federal legislation to pre-empt the field and prevent California from legislating stricter controls.

But our extensive study created new possibilities for legislative action. Just knowing and publicizing the awful dimensions of the problem and the available possible solutions produced massive citizen support and urging from the press to take steps that would never have been contemplated a few months before. We were able to provide facts and citizen support to our congressional delegation in Washington, who were successful in securing a waiver that allows California to go beyond the federal law in enacting stiff controls on auto emissions. (One of our legislative staff is permanently located in Washington, and this close linkage helped us to know exactly what was happening in Washington and how to use our information most effectively.)

Having secured the opportunity to develop our own state smog control law, the Assembly was then able to develop the information required to write such a law and to review the highly technical objections raised by the automobile industry.

During the course of this project, our Assembly Transportation and Commerce Committee, with staff help from the Office of Research, conducted the following activities:

1. Held 5½ days of transcribed hearings at which over fifty witnesses testified. Witnesses included state and national experts on air pollution formation and control and effects of smog on health, agriculture, and the economy.

2. Met and interviewed scores of other persons, including representatives of private industry, the federal Department of Health, Education, and Welfare, the state Air Resources Board, the Department of Public Health, the California Highway Patrol, and the Department of Motor Vehicles.

3. Submitted and evaluated a questionnaire that went to every automobile manufacturer who sold over one hundred cars in California in the past year, requesting detailed information on emission control developments.

4. Visited automobile research facilities, assembly lines, and testing stations in California and Detroit.

5. Reviewed published and unpublished material on vehicle air pollution.

6. Established a mailing list of professional persons and other

citizens (about two thousand names) who are periodically informed of, and invited to comment on, the legislation.

Only after this work was done did the committee write the Pure Air Act of 1968. To assure that the legislation did not demand what was not technologically feasible, the bill was reviewed by a nine-man technical advisory panel of California engineers and scientists, established by the committee for this specific purpose, and chaired by the dean of the School of Engineering at the University of Southern California. The committee also conducted a public forum on smog at which citizens were invited to testify. This provided even greater impetus to enact the very strongest vehicle emission control law in the nation.

Mental Retardation Programs

In several of our projects we have deliberately tried to maximize public involvement prior to the introduction of legislation, rather than waiting for testimony after bills have been introduced. We ask various groups with conflicting views to provide information; we ask interested organizations and industries to gather data for us, using questionnaires we have designed; we distribute preliminary or tentative committee recommendations and structure public hearings to receive feedback and criticism; and we have even prepared rough drafts of actual legislation and submitted them to the affected interests with the request that they criticize and offer alternative language.

When such techniques are used, the legislature stops being an obstacle course for those interested in social change and becomes a facilitating mechanism. To illustrate how these techniques were used with great effectiveness, I will briefly review a project that resulted in a major change in California's mental retardation programs. This project is significant not only because it improved the state's services but because it produced a change that will save millions of dollars. This one project resulted in enough savings to the state taxpayer to pay for the cost of the Assembly's research staff for many years.

Each year, hundreds of families in California plead for help when the problems of caring for their mentally retarded children become overwhelming. And each year the state of California has increased the capacity of its hospitals in response to this pressure. But as California's population grew, and as medical science found new ways of keeping retarded infants alive, the problem of the "waiting list" stubbornly remained. We have grown accustomed to a "waiting list" for state hospitals. The ever-present "waiting list" was tragic testimony to an organizational weakness in state services.

Year after year the legislature appropriated additional funds to eliminate the problem. Since 1955 the support budget for state hospitals for the retarded increased from 15.2 million dollars to over forty-five million dollars. Nevertheless, at almost any time during the past ten years, we had a state hospital "waiting list" of two thousand or more retarded. In 1964 there were over thirteen thousand retarded persons in our state hospitals. To meet the total need for residential care in the traditional manner, the Department of Mental Hygiene has estimated that the state should provide over three thousand new hospital beds during the next four years. The estimated capital outlay for this expansion was 47.6 million dollars. In 1964 plans were in motion to construct these facilities. The department recommended the construction of two thousand of these new hospital beds, and we had already granted seventy-five thousand dollars for working drawings for one five-hundred-bed facility.

If our *only* response to the problem had been the construction of three thousand new beds, by 1968 there would have been sixteen thousand retarded persons in our state hospitals. In addition to the 47.6 million dollars the state would have spent on construction, the yearly support for hospitals for the retarded would have increased by eleven million dollars. But, even if this had been done, we would have accumulated a new "waiting list," and we would now be building again. (New York state, with about the same state population, has twice the number of state hospital beds for the retarded that California does, but New York is also involved in a struggle with a "waiting list.")

Faced with this problem, the Assembly Subcommittee on Mental Health Services conducted the following study:

First, a questionnaire was submitted to each of the state hospitals serving the mentally retarded. The forty-eight-page questionnaire covered every major aspect of the program. During this same period, hospitals were visited and discussions were held with hospital employees, parents with children in the hospitals, and representatives of professional and citizen groups.

Second, the subcommittee conducted a survey of the 225 private facilities licensed to care for the mentally retarded in California.

Third, a questionnaire was submitted to every family in California with a retarded child on the "waiting list" to a state hospital. Through the questionnaire and numerous letters, the subcommittee was able to communicate directly with over twelve hundred families with children on the "waiting list."

What were the subcommittee's findings? We found that less than half of those on the "waiting lists" required state hospital care. We found that over half the families with children on the "waiting list" would not place their children in a state hospital if other alternatives were made available. (A major cause of the lengthy state hospital "waiting lists" stemmed from the fact that despite the needs of children or the desires of their families, the state offered few alternatives other than the state hospital for these retarded children. Each year almost one thousand retarded children were being funneled into a single system, and family finances were a primary factor in determining where these children would go.) We also found that the cost of community care was less than the cost of state hospital care.

Based on these findings, the subcommittee proposed that the State Department of Public Health contract with community agencies, medical centers, and children's hospitals to operate regional centers for the retarded. These regional centers would provide comprehensive diagnosis, and certain families would receive professional guidance *and financial aid* to help them in placing their children in privately operated and state-approved community residential facilities. Financial aid for visiting nurses, homemakers, and babysitters, and day care services would also help many families to keep their children at home.

The committee published a preliminary report describing its findings and conclusions and proposals regarding the problem of the "waiting list." The report was widely publicized and mailed to over one thousand individuals and organizations for the purpose of soliciting reactions and suggestions. Numerous public hearings were held throughout the state, and the committee's proposals were criticized by some, supported by others, and through these discussions they were refined. Then a bill was introduced and passed—and a new program was enacted. The "waiting list" problem is being solved at minimum cost to the taxpayer and much to the satisfaction of the concerned families.

Two new regional centers for the retarded have been operating for over a year now, and eight more are contemplated. During the first year the regional center in Los Angeles, operated under contract with the state by the Los Angeles Children's Hospital, served over five hundred families—230 of them were awaiting admission to the state hospitals. Of these 230, only thirty-nine went on to the state hospitals. The balance are being served in community facilities and in their own homes—with help financed by the state. The average cost is about half the cost of state hospital care. There is no capital outlay. And there is much better integration of the retarded in the mainstream of community life. This does not mean that we will never have to build new state hospitals or improve the old. But it does mean that the use of these hospitals will be limited to those who require long-term care in a medical facility.

Minority Group Unemployment Legislation

Another example of the payoff in legislative research is the approach taken in California's imaginative new legislation to cope with chronic minority group unemployment in the ghetto sections of our state. This project again highlights the problem of relations with the federal government and shows the necessity of legislative initiative on the state level.

For many years now, the federal government has been deeply involved in training and placement programs for the unemployed. In California, federal funds for these programs have increased tenfold. We are now spending over two hundred million dollars a year on these programs.

Twelve months of research has revealed that the old programs do not work. The crazy-quilt of agencies and federal regulations that govern how money is spent in this field guarantees failure. Furthermore, much of the money is not being spent on serving the minority groups concentrated in urban ghetto areas, where the problem is most severe. The unemployed we should be most concerned about do not fit the old definitions. They usually do not qualify for unemployment insurance and they never did. They are not looking for work because they have found that the search for a job is futile.

A special census in 1965 showed that the unemployment rate in south-central Los Angeles was 10.7 percent. This is "official" unemployment—people who have worked, who are available for work, and are actively seeking work. That census also showed 14.8 percent of the males between twenty and sixty-four years of age were "nonparticipants" in the labor force. That is, they were not actively seeking work. In addition, this census revealed that at least 20 percent of the males between twenty and sixty-four could not even be found. If we assume that half the "nonparticipants" are unemployed and that half of those who were not counted in the census were unemployed—and these are both very conservative assumptions—then the male unemployment rate in Los Angeles ghettos stands at 28.1 percent. If we add to this unemployment figure the problem of *underemployment*—those who work only part-time or intermittently—it is quite likely that almost 50 percent of the labor force in our urban ghettos are in need of jobs. And 80 percent of these people are nonwhite. We have no good system for meeting this need.

In preparing legislation, members of the staff visited numerous programs and interviewed the staff and the clients. They found compelling evidence that agency programs are fragmented and uncoordinated; one agency recruits, another orients, a third tests, a fourth teaches, and a fifth places. The odds that a person will drop out or be rejected at any one of these transfer points are extremely high. It is a design for discouragement. The undereducated, unemployed black or Mexican-American who finally summons up the nerve to approach one of our government programs or agencies is beginning a complicated obstacle course. There are dozens of reasons for rejecting him at dozens of points in the process, and dozens of reasons for referring him to other government programs or agencies to start the process over again. In California today there are more than twenty different federally funded programs, each administered by a separate organization, and more such fragmented programs are on the way.

When the facts were clearly known, Democrats and Republicans joined forces to develop corrective legislation. The legislation is not a panacea, but it does hold promise. California will create a new Department of Human Resources Development, independent of our State Department of Employment. This will be a *single* governmental agency where the unemployed person can get the services he needs whether it be training, education, transportation, child care services, or advice on applying for work—in short, whatever it takes to get and keep him on a job.

Within our human resources development agency we propose to locate a number of state agencies that have been created in the past to administer federal and state programs. These agencies are presently unattached to any central agency or are located in some other department that has proven unresponsive to the problems. Thus the new department will include such bodies as our state Office of Economic Opportunity; the Division of Apprenticeship Standards, now within our Department of Industrial Relations; and all the functions of the Manpower Development and Training Act now located in our Department of Employment. The legislation also transfers to a single "Manpower Development Fund" within the state Treasury the many diverse funding sources that now support each of these programs. The new fund will be used by the director of the Department of Human Resources Development, on a priority basis, to solve the problems of the chronically unemployed.

This centralization and decategorization of funds will, for the first time, allow us to use funds to serve those most in need—the minority residents in our ghettos—and to purchase the training and other services they require from any public or private organization. This is a clear departure from the present system of funding various programs and then trying to fit clients into them. We also will create a new kind of civil servant in California, one whose job is defined by the needs of people he serves. Called "job agents," they will be given the responsibility of developing a job plan for each individual enrollee and contracting for the necessary services to make their clients employable, whether it be medical care, babysitting, basic education, or even a suit of clothes for a man who never owned one. The "job agents" will then see to it that the plan actually leads to a job. This approach will require the individual initiative and responsibility that is so sadly lacking in most government programs for the disadvantaged.

The success of this approach depends on cooperation from the federal government in permitting California to utilize federal dollars in a different way.

CONCLUSION

We should not be unduly critical of the federal government. It is understandable how it has come to dominate in so many fields of human concern. We at the state level must have the humility to admit that it was our own neglect that forced Washington to bypass the state in many cases. Many states continue to show little inclination to meet their responsibilities to all their citizens. But when a state shows the initiative to develop its own program, and when the goals of the state program are clearly the same as those of the federal effort, it is in the interest of the nation to put that program into effect. The creativity we all want for our federal system cannot be imposed from above. It must be the result of state, local, and individual effort.

I have tried to show how that effort can be enhanced and the power of state legislatures expanded by equipping them with their own research facilities. Francis Bacon said, "knowledge is power." This is true only when those who have the knowledge also have the ability to *act* on that knowledge. Legislative studies differ from most academic research activities precisely because they are conducted by the legislature—by a decision-making body. As a result, our studies have a vastly greater potential for immediately influencing action.

Legislative studies of important issues can draw upon the information and viewpoints of all the vested interests in the community. It is possible for a legislative study to become a central forum for examining, debating, and solving a problem.

It is possible to break through the barriers that separate the theoreticians from the decision makers. We are showing that a well-informed legislative body can make major policy changes. But there is a caution that should be mentioned. There is no shortcut to developing an informed legislature with the capacity to conceive and enact bold legislation that may conflict with entrenched and time-honored programs. Every legislature is also a kind of bureaucracy, with its own rigid and historical patterns of operation. It takes careful effort to develop a professional staff that understands the intricacies of the legislative process and combines subject-matter skills and political sensitivity. And it takes time for legislators to learn how to use staff effectively.

Legislative bodies can contract with independent research organizations or with academicians in the universities to conduct studies. But if there is insufficient supervision over such outside contracts; if the research is not geared to political realities; and if the legislators are not closely involved in the project so they can develop a good understanding of the elements of the problem, then such studies may merely produce one more expensive report nobody has the time to read.

Expanding the capability of the legislature to provide strong leadership takes time and costs money. But the *underutilization* of legislative power unquestionably leads to wasteful mistakes, the continual weakening of representative government, and public disillusionment in the capacity of government to respond to swiftly changing conditions.

The Consequences
of Legislative Staffing

ALAN ROSENTHAL

The need for legislative improvement is by no means new. Demands for legislative reform are not especially novel. People have been criticizing state legislatures for years. What is unprecedented is that something is now being done. Sermon has given way to action, and real efforts are being made to modernize legislative organization, operations, services, and facilities. Struggles over reapportionment are practically behind. Other struggles are now taking place. Today, legislatures in almost all the states are undergoing change and improvement. As a result, state legislatures are probably better than previously. It may not seem so, because the problems facing them are worse than ever before.

Paradoxically, the rhetoric and logic of reform have not kept pace with reform itself. Nearly everyone agrees as to what the problems are and what should be done. Legislatures maintain too many standing committees and divide their workloads unevenly; committees should be consolidated. Compensation is too little to attract able men; salaries should be increased. Legislatures do not meet often enough to do their jobs; they should convene annually. They are overstaffed and thus inefficient; their size should be reduced. So goes diagnosis; so follows prescription. Yet no one seriously questions whether the patient is being dosed with medicine or a placebo. We are understandably too busy applying the cure to ask what difference, if any, it makes.

If there is any wonder drug in this whole business, it is legislative staffing. Legislatures need greater professional assistance in gathering, processing, and assessing information. Without staff, legislatures cannot possibly arrive at competent judgments, independent of governors, bureaucracies, and interest groups. Without staff, there is little hope of redressing the contemporary imbalance between the power of the legislature on the one hand and that of governors and administrative bureaucracies on the other. Informed opinion is virtually unanimous. The report of the American Assembly, for example, recommends professional staff for majority and minority leaderships, legislative councils, major standing committees, and central services, such as bill drafting, law revision, and library and reference. A recent compilation of recommendations from various national and state reports, published by the Citizens Conference, has more space devoted to staff than to any other subject. My own surveys of opinion among members in six legislatures indicate that staffing is thought to be the most important improvement.

These recommendations make sense. In general, professional staffing does strengthen a legislature. At least this is what I have found in Maryland, Wisconsin, Connecticut, New Jersey, Florida, and Mississippi—the six states in which I have done some work. Staff makes a difference, but what kinds of staff make what kind of difference?

In the best of all possible legislatures, members might expand their staffs as sultans expand their harems. I am prudishly doubtful that this would be wise, even if such a course were conceivable. The fact is that it is not conceivable. With few exceptions, such as in California, legislatures are more constrained than sultans. Competing demands on limited resources restrict legislative opportunities. Just so much money is available; just so much space exists; just so many competent professionals can be recruited. As a consequence, legislators, like everyone else, must consider priorities. First, they must decide how to divide their energies between issues of public policy on the one hand and matters of institutional reform on the other. Second, they must decide how to divide their reform efforts among a number of items, of which staffing is only one. Third, they must decide on the particular type of staff they need most.

The problem is that, while knowledgeable people acknowledge the general effectiveness of legislative staff, they ignore specific effects of particular staffing patterns. The current president of the New York Senate expressed things well when he stated: "To help us in decision-making, we need not just more staff, not just full-time staff, not just better-trained staff, so glibly urged by the traditional reformers." Even more important, he continued, "we need to know what kinds of staff we need." Different species are likely to have impacts that are different in direction and character. One species may affect certain people and aspects of the legislative process, another species may strike alternative targets. Some effects are anticipated, others are unexpected. Some produce radical change, others reinforce traditional habits. Certain results are desirable, others less so.

These are considerations I shall touch upon here. It will not be possible to evaluate every staff at every time in every place. To try to do so would be presumptuous and foolish. Instead, I intend to concentrate on a few staffing patterns and dwell mainly on their effects in the Wisconsin legislature. I shall discuss first how the rank-and-file benefits; second, the ways in which the power of legislative groups is affected; and third, what changes occur in the legislative process as a result.

HOW THE RANK-AND-FILE BENEFITS

Nearly everywhere rank-and-file members of a legislature comprise the lumpen proletariat of government. As a rule, people

expect little of many of them, and many of them expect little
of themselves. Despite occasional bursts of bluster and conten-
tions of confidence, legislators as a class suffer from impoverished
egos and low self-esteem. This is not surprising, since service in a
legislature reminds them constantly of how insignificant an individual is and how small a difference he makes. Whatever may
be said about the importance of their jobs, legislators are rarely
given the help they need in order to contribute very much.

Staff is supposed to help. Nevertheless, few kinds of staff
really offer immediate and tangible benefits to rank-and-file
members. The most notable exception is the bill-drafting service.
Because it is assumed that legislators must introduce bills and
that bills must conform to standards of statutory format and
language, drafting assistance is usually available to ordinary members. Even though deficiencies exist, most legislators have more
contact with and receive more help from bill draftsmen than
from any other type of professional staff. Naturally, then, members feel strongly about expanding such a service. In Connecticut
and Florida, for example, two-thirds of those members we interviewed stated that additional personnel for the bill-drafting
agency should receive the highest priority among staffing possibilities. In New Jersey over half felt this way.

With this exception, rank-and-file members of most state legislatures receive hardly any material assistance at all. Research
bureaus and reference services, which exist in one form or another
in almost every state capitol, do relatively little to meet the day-
to-day needs of legislative back benchers. They devote their
major efforts to routine housekeeping and information services
and the specific demands of party and committee leaders. They
have neither time nor incentive to bother much with requests
from less strategic members. In Wisconsin, for instance, a fiscal
research bureau was established during the 1965 session. One
of its original purposes was to furnish all legislators with relevant
information on budget and tax policy. Quickly, however, the
bureau sensed that its overriding obligation was to the joint

finance committee, which has jurisdiction over appropriations and revenue, and especially to its co-chairmen. Fiscal bureaus in other states, save perhaps the large office of the legislative analyst in California, probably operate in similar fashion, responding to a narrow audience and necessarily neglecting a broader one.

Committee staffs are quite the same. In the U. S. Congress, for example, hundreds of professionals are kept by committees and subcommittees. Yet their attentions are reserved for committee and subcommittee chairmen, and sometimes ranking minority members. Junior members have to look elsewhere. In the states, committee staff does not exist everywhere. Where it does exist, whether on loan from a central research agency or nestled within the bosom of the committee itself, it works to help the few rather than the many. Although they personally stand to gain little, it is interesting that rank-and-file members support the staffing of major standing committees. Among a variety of possibilities, over half the members we interviewed in New Jersey, two-thirds in Connecticut, and three-quarters in Florida considered committee staff to be of highest priority. Apparently they believe that general benefits to the legislature outweigh specific benefits to the individual.

Of greatest direct benefit to individuals are administrative aides. Such assistants, frequently located in home districts, relieve legislators of some of their burdens of publicity, local politics, and constituent problems. This arrangement is supposed to enable the member to spend more time on legislation and committee work. I am not sure whether member time is spent very differently as a result, since so few legislatures provide such help. California has done so for some time and Florida began most recently. However much administrative aides help, it is unlikely that many states will provide for them in the near future. Given the tradition of niggardly support, such an expensive arrangement is just not in the cards. Moreover, other needs are widely believed to deserve higher priority. In Connecticut,

for instance, fewer than one-third of the members felt that administrative aides merited highest priority. In New Jersey fewer
than one-fifth felt this way. In both states, increasing or establishing staffs for party leaders, major committees, fiscal bureaus,
policy research offices, and bill-drafting services were considered
far more important.

In 1965 the Wisconsin legislature created a staffing system
designed to combine service to party leaders, party caucuses,
and individual members of the legislative party. Originally four
full-time research analysts, one for each party in the Assembly
and Senate, were authorized on a pilot basis. Since then, the
arrangement has proven so successful in the view of members
that it has been continued and expanded. The Wisconsin caucus
staffs, I think, should be of great interest to legislators who are
looking for personal help in other two-party states.

Although Wisconsin's caucus staffers do not involve themselves
in district politics or constituent problems, which continue to
be handled by elected politicians, they do provide tangible benefits to party members. First, they help to educate them, by providing political and technical information. Before staffing, the
burden of understanding and explaining bills at caucus meetings
fell on party leaders, who had insufficient energy left to do the
job properly. Analysts took over much of the burden, reviewing
bills on the calendar and reporting to the caucus. In addition,
they turned out periodic newsletters, which were not only informative but entertaining as well. Second, caucus staffers help
members obtain newspaper coverage. A good deal of their time
is devoted to the preparation of press releases, and thus they
directly serve most party members. This makes a difference. My
study of the Wisconsin Assembly indicates an increase in local
press coverage of over 100 percent for both Republicans and
Democrats between 1963 and 1967; much of it was attributable
to the work of caucus staffs. Whether or not increased coverage
made a significant difference in the districts is perhaps less important than the fact that legislators thought it did.

In Wisconsin, two out of three members think the caucus staffs are very effective; most of the others think they are at least somewhat effective. Republicans and Democrats agree, and those members who call on them less are just as likely to rate them highly as those who call on them more. In Wisconsin also, two out of three members believe the fiscal bureau is very effective; the rest believe it at least somewhat effective. There is hardly any difference among Republicans and Democrats on this. In fact, those members who are least affected by their work are just as likely to rate them highly as those who are most affected.

Staff neither reduces a legislator's workload nor provides many material comforts. Although remote from the life of the individual, staff is still appreciated. Not all legislators are equally sold on its merits. Older members, who are more inclined to pursue traditional habits and extol citizen legislatures, are less enamored of staffing than younger members, who are more inclined to try new methods and praise professionalization. To the latter especially, staff provides psychic benefits. It makes them feel that they count. It encourages increased self-confidence and greater pride in legislative service. It provides some degree of stability and security in an arena characterized by reversal and frustration.

THE POWER OF LEGISLATIVE GROUPS

Any change in a legislature is likely to affect somebody's prerogatives, someone's power. Staffing is surely no exception. There is always the danger that part-time legislators will permit full-time staffers to make their decisions for them. The vast majority of staff professionals are neither rash nor reluctant. They respond faithfully, primarily because their survival and success depend on what legislators think of them. Nevertheless, one can think of experienced directors of legislative councils and reference bureaus who control bureaucratic baronies and refuse to budge at all. It is not that the tail wags the dog, but rather that the dog cannot wag the tail. One can think also of ambitious young men who sometimes lead those whom they are employed to obey. Legislators must cope with these types—either bypassing, restraining, nudging, or dislodging them. It may hurt momentarily, but on occasion the dog must nip at the tail or bite the hand that leads it. All it takes is legislative will.

Another danger is less obvious but potentially more serious. It involves not the distribution of power between politicians and bureaucrats but rather the distribution among politicians themselves. Staffing may create or further an imbalance of power within the legislature. Power is relatively centralized in some legislative bodies, with important decisions made by party leaders and caucuses. In others power is relatively decentralized, with important decisions made by standing committees or members on the floor. As far as I can determine, power in most state legislatures is far more centralized than in the houses of the U. S. Congress, since members work only part time, committees hardly work at all, and leaders—often in collaboration with the governor and his aides—exercise predominant control.

A particular staffing arrangement may result in some alteration of the balance of power. This is not necessarily harmful. But the probabilities of who gets what, when, and how should be considered before a legislature decides on one type of staff rather than another. Legislative generalists serving individual members, subject-matter specialists serving standing committees, and legislative politicos serving party leaders and/or party caucuses will probably have different effects. The first group will enhance the capability of individuals, the second will add to the strength of committees, and the third will increase the power of party leaderships.

Let me give flesh to these assertive bones by again referring to Wisconsin. In comparison to other states, legislative power in Wisconsin is centralized. It is held mainly by party leaders and caucuses. On matters of revenue and appropriations, the joint finance committee, dominated by the speaker's appointments, is also strong. Recently it has been strengthened even further as the result of the establishment of a fiscal bureau to serve as its staff. Most legislators agree that fiscal staff made a big difference to the committee. Other committees, however, are weak. They have received little staff assistance. Over the years the authority of committees has declined. One reason is the increased sophistication of younger legislators, who no longer took their cues from standing committees. Another reason is the new caucus staffs, which provided alternative sources of information to party members.

My study of Wisconsin confirms that caucus staffs help solidify the legislative party, and, perhaps most important, buttress party leaders. This is best illustrated by the work of Democratic staffers in the assembly, who proved particularly helpful to minority leaders. They publicized leadership positions and activities, giving them far greater coverage than before in the capital city press. They fronted for leaders, performing some of the more obnoxious tasks and taking the heat from the rank-and-file for unpopular leadership decisions or mistakes in judgment or timing. They functioned as a channel for complaints, which members were reluctant to bring personally to their leaders. They acted as the "eyes and ears" of leaders, informing them of the mood of the legislative party, letting them know when things were going smoothly or when storms were brewing in caucus, and advising them as to who needed persuasion and what persuasive techniques would work on whom. Caucus staff in Wisconsin certainly helped individual legislators and undoubtedly led to some increase in their independence from committee recommendations. But at the same time it provided leaders with tools to increase their influence over the caucus. Concurrently, fiscal staff added to the influence of the joint finance committee. Both staffs, however, contributed to a relative decline in the power of substantive committees in the legislature.

I doubt that Wisconsin legislators anticipated these developments. Each legislature should consider the possibilities; each must decide for itself. I personally think that some balance in the internal distribution of power is desirable. If so, then those legislatures, such as New Jersey, Pennsylvania, and New York, where power is already highly centralized, might devote more attention to strengthening committees. Those, such as New Hampshire, Montana, and Mississippi, where power is relatively decentralized, might devote more attention to strengthening legislative leaders or legislative parties. Intelligent choices in staffing is one method of achieving balance. It will not be easy, because this is the type of situation where the squeaky wheel does not get the grease. Groups who have power are likely to get staff, and staff, in turn, is likely to confer greater power on those who are already powerful. Legislators should guard against this—they should preserve their strong points and strengthen their weak ones.

CHANGES IN THE LEGISLATIVE PROCESS

In advocating increased professional staff, both those inside and outside the legislature have as their goal a change in the process by which lawmakers conduct their affairs. Legislators themselves usually have modest expectations. They hope that additional help will lighten the legislative burden and increase legislative efficiency. They do not really envisage any revolutionary transformation. Academics and consultants are more ambitious, since they are less likely to suffer the constraints of reality. They too advocate lesser burdens and more efficiency, but are inclined also to contemplate radical change, substituting new legislative processes for old ones. As often as not, these anticipations are not confirmed, and the ways in which staffing affects the legislative process are quite unexpected.

Staffing certainly does not reduce workload. In fact, additional staff in reference bureaus, bill-drafting offices, and other such agencies will probably expand the volume of work. As

Norman Meller, a political scientist, speculated, there is a possibility indeed "that Parkinson's law governs, and work requested of legislative service agencies expands to meet the growth of staff, rather than the reverse." Committee staffs also make more work. If Congress can serve as an example, then the more competent the staff, the more problems and opportunities it will uncover, the more alternatives it will examine, and the more information and research it will pass on to a committee. Hence, more committee work.

Nor does staff make for greater efficiency, especially if efficiency means getting the job done with less effort and resources. If, however, efficiency means better methods by which legislatures reach informed policy decisions, things must be seen from another perspective. I suspect that the results are generally good, but not always in accord with intentions. What happened in Wisconsin as a consequence of caucus and fiscal staffing offers some interesting clues to staff impact on the legislative process.

Whatever Wisconsin's leaders had in mind when they established caucus staffs, some potential effects were probably overlooked. The promotion of greater intraparty unity and interparty conflict were not anticipated. As I have already mentioned, staffs strengthened leadership, and in doing so they solidified the legislative parties. The minority staff especially tried to: convince members that their individual fortunes and party fortunes were linked together; provide members with arguments for following the leadership, particularly on platform bills; prevent members from personal embarrassment or attack; and stave off intraparty disputes and factional disagreements. Its efforts made a difference; the minority party united, and the majority closed ranks in response.

Caucus staffing also led to increased controversy over legislative alternatives to administration proposals. A number of alternatives were prepared by the minority staff. On most issues, which the Democrats could not hope to win, the major outcome was increased public awareness of contention between two points of view. In a number of instances, however, the minority did influence the legislative process. It attacked an administration proposal, provoked public response, peeled off a few Republican votes, and persuaded the majority to modify its position. Sometimes the minority succeeded in killing a measure; sometimes it forced a compromise. In all of this, staff made a difference.

In establishing fiscal staff, Wisconsin's leaders contemplated an agency that would reinforce the legislature's customary budgetary role. They had no grandiose scheme in mind, but only hoped that a fiscal bureau would help the legislature do better what it had been doing before. By contrast, an expert consultant working for the legislature contemplated that fiscal staff would promote major change in the very nature of legislative fiscal review. He hoped that staff would contribute to a far more rational-comprehensive consideration of the state budget, including examination of fiscal alternatives, an understanding of the total budget, and long-range analysis and planning.

The results thus far appear more in line with the expectations of legislative leaders than with those of the expert consultant. The fiscal staff is still too small to cover the entire budget; instead, it concentrates its efforts. Because its effectiveness depends on the avoidance of the political thicket and the brambles of partisan issues, it provides little in the way of major alternatives to administration proposals. Because the finance committee is interested in the immediate, operating from election to election, the staff focuses on the here and now and neglects planning for an uncertain political and economic future. In short, the staff has adopted the colors of the legislature, and not galloped into battle with a standard of its own.

Despite its moderation, the fiscal bureau has had considerable impact. It is true that in relation to the magnitude of state spending, the effects of a legislature are limited. But, within these limits, staff has given valuable support to the finance committee. In the 1967 session, for example, of its seventy written recommendations on the budget, twenty-nine were accepted in precisely the form proposed and another fourteen were accepted with some modification by the committee. Staff has helped the committee in its efforts to economize—eliminating waste, duplication, and a few old programs that had outlived their usefulness. In the 1967 session, budgetary cuts of approximately 3.8 million dollars—mainly in higher education and public welfare, where staff concentrated its attention—could be directly attributed to the fiscal bureau. An additional 5.7 million dollars in budget reductions were certainly indirect consequences of its suggestions.

Changes in the legislative process as a consequence of partisan and fiscal staffing were hardly revolutionary. Caucus staff simply strengthened legislative partisanship, which was already quite strong. Fiscal staff simply strengthened legislative budget-cutting, which was already first on the agenda of the finance committee. I would guess that in other states, as well as in Wisconsin, increased staffing reinforces the legislative process, but does not transform it. Ordinarily, staff professionals do not rock the boat; they adapt to the course set by those for whom they crew. This is what is expected of them, what is convenient for them, and what is rewarding to them.

Whether or not these results are desirable can be disputed. Evaluation will vary, according to one's view of what the legislature is all about. Perhaps increased partisan conflict is not healthy, particularly in a system where partisanship is already a way of life. However, I personally believe that most legislatures can tolerate conflict, especially when the majority party is aligned with the executive branch. Perhaps greater economizing makes less sense than a comprehensive comparison of all existing programs and available alternatives, for the future as well as the present. I am rather doubtful that the latter can be done, although increased rationality is surely possible. Nevertheless, supporting the capacity for stinginess of an appropriations committee is extremely important, since practically everyone else— the governor, departments and agencies, interest groups, and even substantive standing committees—is expansionist, program-oriented, and disposed to spend money by increasing demands on the state's purse.

CONCLUSION

Factors other than staffing also affect the strength of state legislatures. Salaries, facilities, and the length and timing of legislative sessions may be among them. It is difficult to isolate the effects of one, since legislatures that have made a single improvement usually have made others as well. Yet, of all the factors over which a legislature has some measure of control, staff is most important. It is no panacea, however. Staff in Wisconsin did not make a weak legislature strong; rather it made a strong legislature stronger. Staffs in other states will not make mountains out of molehills; but they will change the shape of the terrain.

State legislatures must improve their staffs, if they hope to improve themselves. This can be done. Legislators simply must try to anticipate what will happen if they create a new staff here or augment an old one there. Thinking in terms of workload and efficiency is not satisfactory. Far more is involved. It requires legislators to take into account the potential advantages and disadvantages of one arrangement in comparison with another, so that they can get the types of staff that will serve them most effectively.

Unicameralism—
The Wave of the Future

JESS UNRUH

The most effective way to improve state government and to rejuvenate the federal system is the consolidation of state legislatures into one house each. The present two-house system is a costly and inefficient anachronism that thwarts the popular will, caters to private interests, and hobbles responsible and responsive decision-making. The model state constitution prepared by the National Municipal League begins the legislative article with this comment:

> The purposes of [this provision] are to permit the development of a legislature with sufficient power to formulate policy in response to the needs of the state, a legislature in which the seats are distributed fairly, a legislature which has high "visibility" performing its duties responsibly and in such a fashion that the public can oversee and judge its actions, a legislature where the majority rules while affording protection against arbitrary action, and a legislature that has sufficient time and resources for informed deliberation. Such a legislature should provide opportunities for public service attractive to the most competent citizens.

The National Municipal League recommends that the legislature be composed of a *single* chamber.

Unless unicameralism is made central to the present efforts to reform and modernize state legislatures, I do not believe that increased salaries, new facilities, and professional staff will be more than temporary palliatives for the ills that it is hoped they will cure. These reforms in themselves only make a more efficient horse and buggy. I take little comfort from the fact that legislatures can be the fastest horse and buggy in the jet age.

With all respect to the political scientists, unicameralism is a word that puts many people off. It carries a ring of inside professional knowledge beyond the understanding of the usual person. Instead, think of the legislature as the board of directors of a state, the governor as the executive director, and the citizens as shareholders. The analogy can be pressed too far, but it is substantially accurate—especially at a time when General Motors shareholders are forming factions and using their proxies to push the board into new areas of public policy. Does any corporation have *two* boards of directors? Would there be any point to it? But then most people would agree that the business of a corporation demands a clear decision-making capability. Why should we expect less of state legislatures?

CYCLES OF INEFFICIENCY

One can also approach the question straight on: What are the roles of the state legislature supposed to be? Let me briefly suggest that the legislature should: (1) pose questions and choices concerning public policy; (2) focus public attention on important issues; (3) determine the allocation of public resources; and (4) exercise oversight over the entire range of governmental affairs.

The legislature is both a deliberative body and an arena for the resolution of conflict. Unicameralism will permit state legislatures to perform these roles, and to do so 1000 percent more successfully than now. There are many actions that a one-house legislature could take that are presently difficult or impossible with two houses. I doubt that the purposes of a legislature, however they are understood, are served by any of the expensive, trivial, byzantine, and maddening convolutions that the presence of two houses creates for anyone who is trying to get an issue heard or a bill passed. Consider also the enormous amounts of time that these maneuverings consume. I will give you a few examples from the California Legislature.

The California budget probably occupies more time than any other legislative matter. Here is the cumbersome route it follows through the legislature. It is introduced in the same form in both houses. It then is sent to the finance committee of each house. There it consumes most of the time of 25 to 30 percent of the members of each house for from four to five months, and sometimes longer. It also consumes the bulk of the time of the best-paid Assembly and Senate staff employees. But this is only the visible and expected part of the iceberg. The budget draws the major part of the staff time of the top people in the governor's department of finance, who scurry back and forth between the Assembly ways and means committee and the Senate finance committee. Each executive department whose budget is being scrutinized also sends representatives to these two committees and their many subcommittees. The third house [lobbyists] and interested citizens groups also have to cover both houses.

Yet this is really all shadow boxing, because the budget is finally written by three senators and three assemblymen in a so-called free-conference committee, and the product of their labors and decisions may bear little relationship to the budget passed by either house. The days (sometimes weeks) of labor that these six members contribute again require the attendance of the top staff people of the Legislative Analyst's office and the department of finance.

It is just as bad with other legislation. School finance bills must be sent first to the education committees, then to the finance committees, then to the floor, and then the whole maddening process is repeated again in the other house. This requires representatives of executive agencies, legislative staff, and affected interests to appear at every repetitive step of the way. And, again, the final bill may well be written in a free-conference committee of six members to resolve the disputes between the houses, or to do *whatever else* comes into their minds. And there can be yet another level of committee operation in this mess—the joint committee, which is almost beyond anyone's control. The need for these committees would be totally eliminated if there were a one-house legislature.

Most of the more vicious log-rolling and log-jamming in the legislative process comes about between the two houses. The California Senate finance committee for years has had a practice of holding all Assembly bills until the last few days of the session to keep a bargaining lever over members of the lower house. With that excuse gone the chairman of a one-house finance committee would be hard put to hold all appropriation measures until the last ten days.

THE COSTS OF BICAMERALISM

This pattern of inefficiency is all too familiar; it is repeated in a hundred different ways in all forty-nine bicameral legislatures in this country. Yet I do not advocate unicameralism simply to achieve neatness in government organization. I favor unicameralism because I believe that it would improve the legislature's competitive position with respect to other branches of government. A shift to unicameral legislatures is at the heart of legislative reform. I agree with the political scientist who said: "The outstanding feature of unicameralism is that it affords a better setting in which to effect other legislative reforms." All of them are more likely to occur, and will be more effective, when implemented in a unicameral system.

The expense of the cycle of inefficiency described earlier is incredible. Legislatures today spend on their own services only a very tiny amount of state budgets. In California it is less than one-half of 1 percent. Under a bicameral system the duplication of cost in terms of staff time and legislator time is enormous. Experience tells us that taxpayers are usually not willing to pay the full cost for an effective legislature. I suspect that a one-house legislature of around a hundred members could save as much as 30 to 40 percent of the present two-house costs in California and that most other states could show comparable savings. These savings could pay a significant portion of the more costly reforms such as professional staff, modern facilities, and compensation required to keep able lawmakers in the legislature. Obviously, the executive branch would also save considerably in dealings with a unicameral legislature. The expenses of business and public groups that have to appear before the legislature could also be cut accordingly.

I believe that unicameralism is the long-term solution to many of the problems now plaguing state legislatures, particularly in the smaller states where the argument is so consistently made that they cannot afford to provide their legislatures with the proper decision-making tools.

ACCOUNTABILITY AND VISIBILITY

But I do not wish to suggest a penny-pinching approach to federalism. What I am really concerned with is responsible decision-making power at the state level. Two-house legislatures neutralize the force of the legislature in state government. Governors can, and do, arrange alignments of one house against the other over pieces of legislation and programs. This kind of whipsaw technique can ensure the defeat of legislation, even though it may be supported by the majority of legislators. In my opinion, the committee system provides opportunity enough for governors and for special-interest groups to exert pressure on legislatures. When one house is pitted against the other, a serious power vacuum—one that outsiders are all too eager to fill—is created. With only one house, however, the legislature would more nearly match the unified structure of the executive branch and, therefore, be a more worthy competitor.

When a smart governor plays one house against the other, the public can rarely identify where the responsibility for defeat of legislation lies. The public can rarely detect the real culprit.

In addition, the press might do a much better and more thorough job covering the legislative process, and pinpointing responsibility, if there were only one-third as many committees functioning.

What legislators desperately need today is visibility. Visibility promotes competence in, and attracts talent to, the legislative arena. What the public needs is to be able to fix responsibility. I do not believe that we can expect the public to support state government until the public has this capability. But consider the citizen's problem. He currently has an assemblyman and a state senator. They may well be in direct disagreement about a measure the voter is interested in. Whose word does he take as to what has happened to his interests? And who is really "representing" his point of view?

The National Municipal League points out that: "If a bicameral system is retained, population should be the basis for representation in both houses, but differences in size of districts and differences in the length of terms can provide different constituencies and give each house distinctive characteristics that will avoid making one a mere carbon copy of the other." I suggest that honest, accurate apportionment will invariably make the houses near carbon copies of each other. The degree to which the houses differ may well be the measure by which reapportionment has been unfair or dishonest.

Since the "one-man, one-vote" ruling, no legitimate reason for two-house legislatures remains today, for anyone except those special interests who over the years have gained advantage for themselves and who now are interested in preserving a system that provides as many obstacles to change as possible. Whether you agree with my assessment or not, it must be admitted that the imposition of the "one-man, one-vote" formula has made serious consideration of unicameralism far more realistic than previously.

Bicameralism in the legislative branch may be an indicator of the degree to which legislatures have failed to keep up with the trends in American government. In local government, bicameral legislative bodies have virtually disappeared, although they were once a common feature of city and county government. Today's bicameral state legislature is still functioning essentially as it did 120 years ago. That was hardly adequate then—it is woefully, tragically improper today.

Unicameralism may also offer the best hope for our tripartite system to survive as a democratic form of government. If state legislatures are to play a significant role in twentieth-century American government, such basic kinds of reforms must be implemented and within the very near future. If this does not occur, I doubt rather seriously that legislatures or state governments in general will be an effective instrument of the people's will. The states (and certainly the state legislatures) will simply be bypassed in favor of a not very responsive federal government.

CONCLUSION

Single-house legislatures will only happen if members and people who are involved in the process and committed to its success think that unicameralism is worth working for. Look at the state legislature from the point of view of the member. How much time do members spend on interhouse squabbles that should be spent on policy deliberations within their own house? Are committees in one house passing out bad bills so that the other house will have to take the heat for killing them? Are members stalling bills from the other house in order to gain leverage to get their own bills through? Do they create unwieldy joint committees in an attempt to get around the problems of two houses, only to get Frankenstein's monsters as a result? Is the third house playing legislators off against their colleagues in the other house, so that legislation on which both houses basically agree goes down the tubes? Is the governor doing the same? Look at the state legislature from the point of view of a citizen. Does he see charges of interhouse bill highjacking and name calling? Does he, or anyone else, know who speaks with authority on questions involving major new legislation? Would he know where his testimony on such legislation would get the fairest hearing? Would he, as a taxpayer, be inclined to give legislators the salary, staff, and facilities that are needed to do the job?

By now the rest of the questions are obvious. The answers should leave one with a clearer understanding of why many people in this nation have concluded that the system cannot produce answers any more. These people are proposing solutions of their own: burn the whole country down and start over; abolish the states; drop out; or turn it over to Washington.

If the states are the critical link in the federal system, we in state government should have solutions too. If the federal system is worth saving, people at the state level are going to have to give it a lot of help. In every state constitution I have ever seen the legislative article precedes the executive. I take this to mean that the drafters believed in the importance of a strong and responsive legislature. If the constitution has to be amended to make the legislature unicameral, then members themselves will have to carry the ball. There are a lot of people who can help. The National Municipal League has offices throughout the country. The Committee for Economic Development is a national organization of businessmen that has endorsed single-chamber state legislatures. The Citizens Conference on State Legislatures has a successful record of helping state legislators and citizens to improve and modernize legislative operations.

What is needed now is for risk takers in the public arena to take the work of these groups and others and translate it into action. This sounds like a tough process in a state where long months or years have to be spent struggling to get even modest reforms. It is. But we should all keep in mind the words of the designer of Chicago's Outer Drive and park system in the past century. He was a dreamer who won against the odds, just as we must if the federal system is going to survive in this century. He wrote:

> Make no little plans; they have no magic to stir men's blood and probably themselves will not be realized. Make big plans; aim high in hope and work, remembering that a noble, logical diagram once recorded will never die, but long after we are gone will be a living thing, asserting itself with ever-growing insistency.

part two

THE VIEWS OF EXECUTIVE
AND LEGISLATIVE LEADERS

The Views of Executive and Legislative Leaders An Introduction

ALAN ROSENTHAL

It is curious indeed that although American state legislatures have made considerable progress in recent years, their fears of subordination and obsolescence have continued to increase. State legislators throughout the nation are concerned—some verge on paranoid—about the lingering power of the federal government or the dominance of governors and executive agencies, or both. National power and the ascendancy of state executives, it would appear, go hand in hand. The former encourages the latter. National programs, and particularly federal grants-in-aid, whether administered by local jurisdiction or by departments and agencies of state government, tend to strengthen other institutions at the expense of the state legislature. Instead of responding with a sense of urgency, state legislatures have witnessed their own eclipse almost helplessly.

I

The views of executive and legislative leaders, which appear in Part Two of this volume, deal primarily with themes of the federal and executive challenges to the independence of state legislatures. In his essay, for example, Jess Unruh, on the basis of his experience as Speaker of the California Assembly, president of the National Conference of State Legislative Leaders, member of the Advisory Commission on Intergovernmental Relations, and champion of legislative reform, comments on the threats to the legislature of federal power and gubernatorial dominance. The perspectives of other leaders—governors as well as legislators—suggest reasons why the legislative role is diminished and how it can be revitalized. The advice of United States Senator Harold E. Hughes, who served as governor of Iowa from 1963 through 1968, is most pertinent. Senator Hughes calls for a new and constructive dialogue between the branches of government and between the levels of government. "We need," he writes, "to listen, give ground, eat crow, negotiate, conciliate, and do whatever is necessary to preserve our federal system." Too often, however, disputants have talked past one another rather than with one another and have gone to the periphery rather than to the core of issues in contest.

Despite the rhetoric of the new federalism, talk of strengthening the capacity of the states, and proposals for revenue sharing, much remains to be done before the federal system returns to equilibrium. Much, in fact, will have to be done by the states themselves; for it is their past neglect of their own responsibilities, as much as anything else, that has prompted the federal government to act decisively. Harold E. Hughes makes the case against the states most forcefully. He is extremely critical of both governors and legislatures who complain loudly about the erosion of states' rights "without really demonstrating either the imagination or initiative to do anything to strengthen the state's role." Governors, with only a few exceptions, have come a long way. Republicans and Democrats alike are now responding to the challenges posed in Washington, and are beginning to confront the environmental, educational, social, and urban issues of the day.

State legislatures, with only a few exceptions, have been more recalcitrant. In the past, they proved negligent in recognizing the problems of the cities and other communities. As Senator Hughes maintains in his criticism of the legislature for not sharing state revenues, "it is generally the legislature that wins the blue ribbon for obliviousness to local governments' financial needs." Even now, state legislatures find it difficult to deal competently with the initiatives of the federal government. Reflecting on Iowa, the senator recalls that by and large, "the legislature could be counted on to be hostile toward anything that came from Washington."

Such attitudes and behavior are typical of many states. Only recently, for instance, the under secretary of the Department of Health, Education, and Welfare discussed President Nixon's family assistance plan at a conference of fifty-six state legislative leaders from thirteen western states. His intention was not only to convey information, but also to engender support for the Administration bill, which after passing the House of Representatives had become stalled in the finance committee of the U. S. Senate. The reactions of legislative leaders—Democrats and Republicans, from larger and smaller states—were practically uniform. For them the paramount consideration was not what the Administration believed the family assistance programs would accomplish, but rather what it would cost their states. Despite assurances to the contrary, suspicions that the program would overtax the financial abilities of the states could not be allayed. In part because of past obligations incurred by the acceptance of federal programs and funds, distrust of the federal government had become deeply entrenched. Such attitudes are understandable, but they constitute a poor foundation for a new federalism.

Not all of the fault today lies with the states, nor even with state legislatures. Federal officials, and particularly those in the career service, have expended little effort consulting with leaders in the states. Only occasionally have they been seriously mindful of state views. Even congressmen, many of whom have served in state legislatures, have become federalized quickly. Although responsive to opinion in their districts, they have given little heed to the views of leadership in their states. Governors and state legislative leaders are trying hard to remedy the situation, to increase communications between levels of government. At their conferences—whether national, regional, or party—governors talk constantly about their state's relationships with the federal government. The subject is also on the agenda of conferences held by legislative leaders and rank-and-file members. Governors have established state offices in Washington; some legislatures have done the same. Now, legislative leaders, spurred by Robert P. Knowles, president pro tem of the Wisconsin Senate, are trying to devise ways of sharing representation in the nation's capital, of receiving information regarding federal programs more rapidly, and of having greater impact on the congressional delegations from their states.

There is promise in all this. Hope exists that more states will take on an innovative role. Indeed, the history of American federalism has been studded by examples of innovation by several states, which have served as laboratories for experimentation and facilitators of nationwide change. Wisconsin has blazed numerous trails, many of which have been followed by other states and by the federal government as well. Recently, California has been in the forefront. It is of critical importance that the federal government encourage and abet creativity by the states. Yet this has been difficult to achieve. In its endeavors to raise the standards of many states, the federal government limits the standards of some others. Arthur Bolton, in his essay included in Part One, notes how this occurred with respect to California's program to set rigid criteria regulating automobile pollutants. In Part Two, Jess Unruh, from the perspective of the legislative leader's position, also considers the problem. His conclusion is clear. "In a state that has demonstrated a capacity to initiate and carry out effective programs," he writes, "federal legislation should permit the state government to control and further specify the way in which federal monies should be used."

II

Even if legislatures manage to establish productive relationships with the federal government, they still face the task of establishing satisfactory relationships with their own governors and executive bureaucracies. The challenge here is for the legislature to maintain its independence, and deal with the executive branch from a position of equal strength, responsibility, and competence.

Take the question of legislative strength. By "strength" we mean the power of the legislature as compared to that of the executive over the determination of state policy and the conduct of state government. It is commonly believed that the legislature is subservient to the executive branch. But often this has not been the case. There are a number of legislatures that have been at least equal in strength to the executive. Arizona, California, Colorado, Florida, Minnesota, Mississippi, Nebraska, South Carolina, and Wisconsin (and perhaps others) have had truly coequal legislatures, as far as power in comparison to the executive is concerned. Legislatures in other states—such as Alabama, Connecticut, Illinois, Louisiana, New Jersey, New York, Ohio, and Virginia—have been less than equal.

The strength of a legislature depends to some extent on the partisan or factional distribution of power in a state. Frequently, a legislature controlled by one party can be expected to take a harder line when the executive branch is controlled by the

other party. But the division of partisan control does not necessarily engender legislative strength. In some states, such as
New York and New Jersey, the governor has been able to
dominate despite opposition party control of the legislature.
In others, such as Wisconsin and California, governors have
encountered considerable difficulty even when their party controlled the other branch. In his essay, Harold E. Hughes points
out that in Iowa a governor, with his party holding a majority
in the legislature, was not assured of success with his legislative
program. "The apartheid between the governor and the legislature," he posits, "is deeper than party differences."

The "apartheid" Hughes mentions is based largely on features
of the political system, established in the past and continuing
into the present. The most significant feature is the party or
factional system of the state. Generally, where parties, as organized
throughout the state, are strong or factions persistent, the power
of the executive will be enhanced at the expense of that of the
legislature. Governors as political leaders take advantage of party
or factional organization, and state, county, or local parties or factions make their appeals to and receive their rewards from governors. The party and executive reinforce one another, and the
legislature's influence is secondary. By contrast, where party or
factional organization is weak (very often in states where the
progressive tradition is strong), power tends to be more dis-
persed and the legislature becomes a more important arena for
the actual—as well as the symbolic—determination of policy.

In his essay, Governor Richard B. Ogilvie, who began his
term as chief executive of Illinois in 1969, discusses how the
partisan political system helps shape executive and legislative
institutions. He states that "institutional factors in the political
system of the state may severely restrict or limit the actual operations of the legislature." In Illinois, he notes, Democratic legislators from Cook County regard loyalty to the county party organization higher than loyalty to the district or to the legislature
itself. The leaders of the political parties—and not members of

the legislature—are the focal point for the resolution of major conflicts. This makes it difficult for the legislature to play a creative, innovative role. By contrast, for Republicans the legislature is a real, representative forum. But the tension between the two parties' views of the legislative role—with each party unable to use the other's methods—detracts from political decision-making in the state.

Dependent as it is on rather durable characteristics of the political system, the power of legislatures has not been subject to rapid change. Nevertheless, today more than ever before, political features that once seemed frozen are undergoing substantial change. Nearly everywhere, party organization is declining and partisan affiliation is waning. In many states real opportunity exists for the legislature, in improving itself, to exercise great influence on a political system that previously had so completely determined legislative life. In Connecticut, for example, the legislature's long tradition was one of acquiescence to gubernatorial and state party leadership. Since 1967, however, the legislature has begun to transform itself, and in the process is reshaping the party and political systems of the state.

III

Legislative equality in terms of strength is one thing; equality of responsibility and competence is quite another. There are strong legislatures (at least as compared to their own executives) that are nonetheless irresponsible and incompetent. Problems of legislative responsibility and competence are what executive and legislative leaders believe to be of utmost importance.

Carl E. Sanders, who served as Georgia's governor from 1963 through 1966, goes further. In his essay he compares the two institutions of state government: "The executive branch has moved ahead to try to cope with the times; the legislative branch has talked a good game, but somehow has not managed to keep up." However sympathetic he may be, Governor Sanders lays the blame squarely on his state's legislature. He describes the budgeting process in the state, recounting how the executive had staffed itself, while seven years after a 1962 budget act the Georgia General Assembly still had not hired the budget analyst it had authorized itself. In 1968 the legislature for the first time in years seriously challenged the governor's budget, but had to turn to the executive for information. Even then, the appropriations committee was neither organized nor staffed to receive the necessary budget information and to act on it. Governor Sanders believes that the legislature should be accorded higher status and greater respect. But, he concludes, "before the public is going to go along with buying admittedly expensive improvements, it is going to have to be convinced that state legislatures are doing a top-notch job with what they already have." Such a case will not be easy for many legislatures to make, but it can be done.

Legislatures will have to work harder and operate with more visibility than they do currently. This may be one of the chief benefits offered by annual sessions. In Harold E. Hughes' view, legislatures have governed not so much by legislating as by *not* legislating. With annual sessions, or at least with more frequent meetings, legislatures will have more time to get things done. Furthermore, with annual sessions people will be aware of the existence of the legislature, critical of its failures, and more demanding of constructive action. Charles F. Kurfess, a Republican member of the Ohio House of Representatives since 1957 and Speaker since 1967, agrees, noting that a major advantage of annual sessions is that the legislature can examine fiscal policy, even though there is a biennial budget, and committees can operate far more effectively.

To Speaker Kurfess an increase in legislative work does not mean a full-time legislature. He is not in favor of fully professional legislatures, since citizen legislators engaged in outside vocations have a better ability to "feel the pulse" of their districts. "I am satisfied," he writes, "that the so-called part-time legislator with adequate staffing can actually perform a better job than perhaps most of us could perform on a full-time basis." The issue of professional versus citizen legislatures is not the real issue. In most states, most legislators will continue to be part-time for some years to come. However, some members, such as elective leaders and committee chairmen, may be expected to work on practically a full-time basis. And standing committees, instead of meeting only when the legislature is in actual session, may be expected to meet periodically and work effectively throughout the year.

More work is extremely important, but still not enough. People, who are represented by members of a house and senate, should be informed of what the legislature is doing and of the choices before it. One of the greatest values of representative assemblies is that they provide an arena in which members with conflicting orientations and interests can educate one another and the tolerance of diversity can be fostered. Jess Unruh, in his essay from the leader's position, remarks on the state legislature "as a meeting place, as a place of negotiation, and as a place for developing understanding among suburbanites and city-dwellers, among socio-economic classes, and among racial and ethnic groups." But understanding is really meaningful only if it is communicated from representatives to their constituents, so that each and every citizen can benefit by having his own predispositions challenged by those of others. Charles F. Kurfess stresses the necessity for legislators to inform their constituents of the concerns and potential problems they face, the alternative courses open, and the reasons for selecting one course in preference to others. The education of legislators is important; the education of the public is vital.

There is another important point, which is raised by Richard B. Ogilvie. Many legislatures, despite improvement in organization and procedures, are not really turning out a much improved work product. A major reason, according to the Illinois governor, is that members of these legislatures do not view their role as seeking out problem areas of public concern and searching for solutions. Instead, they view themselves as judges reaching verdicts after contestants argue in adversary proceedings. In addition, many legislators do not even want to make controversial decisions. The consequence is that controversial proposals and innovative solutions are left to others, and frequently to the executive branch.

IV

Legislatures will have to work out their relationships with the chief executive in order for each to participate most effectively in shaping state policies and state programs. Here, too, more effort, by means of annual sessions or otherwise, may help. As Harold E. Hughes mentions, annual sessions will increase understanding and cooperation between the executive and legislative branches—if only because the two branches "will be forced into a closer togetherness." Togetherness and coziness are not the same. "The governor and the lawmakers should respect one another and understand one another's prerogatives better than they do," writes Senator Hughes, "but if the proper separation of powers is to be preserved, they should not be too fraternal." This makes excellent sense, although it may be difficult to achieve in practice.

The problem is that frequently the governor takes the legislative leaders to his bosom, and together they are responsible for the formulation of a program. Far more often than not, however, it is the governor and executive branch who formulate the program and the legislative leaders who are co-opted and assent. Some cooperation between the branches is obviously needed. But what is especially bothersome about this close relationship is that while it may increase the personal, political status of a few leaders, it does nothing at all for the legislature. The legislature remains as before, deprived of any independent leadership. Speaker Kurfess has this in mind when he cautions that leaders should not be satisfied that by virtue of their positions they are deeply involved in the important policy decisions of government. They should ensure, he urges, that rank-and-file legislators are deeply involved too.

The type of situation where leaders and the executive together deal with a supine legislature is common in a number of states. Not in Wisconsin, however, where except for Phillip LaFollette, who was governor in the 1930s and who exerted the most forceful and intimate leadership, the separation of powers has been observed scrupulously. Warren P. Knowles filled the office of governor from 1965 through 1970. During this period, he always had the benefit of a Republican majority in the state Senate and generally of one in the state Assembly also. Nevertheless, in his essay included here, he declares it virtually impossible for a governor and his own legislative leadership to formulate a program. In Governor Knowles' view, "the chief executive must present the administration program as he sees it and then let the legislature act accordingly." It is up to the leaders to eventually come around in support of the administration's legislative program.

To responsibly support, or oppose, or modify, or substitute for an administration's program, a legislature should deal from a position of strength. This means, to some extent at least, a united legislative front. Staffing, Jess Unruh points out, can lead to increased cooperation between the legislative parties. "When each party can participate jointly in the origination and development of a program and feel it has a stake in it," he writes, "not only is the program's legislative road smoothed, but gubernatorial hostility is neutralized." Assistance is extremely important for the legislative minority, because "with staff and facilities, the minority can move intelligently, dissect proposals of the majority, and offer constructive amendment rather than simple obstinate obstruction." Governor Knowles, by contrast, is doubtful. Staff assistance, in his opinion, "is not a substitute for hard work. . . . is not a panacea for the frustrations of legislatures." Having observed a caucus staff promote partisanship, he is critical, particularly of the "outpromise" game of the minority party.

Strengthening the legislature so that it can be an equal partner in government does not necessarily mean reducing the power of the executive branch. Governor Knowles indicates that he is disturbed by the implication that the best way to strengthen legislatures is to weaken executives. Speaker Kurfess of Ohio generally agrees. "I would think," he writes, "that a legislature can be a more effective body and play a broader role without seeking to weaken the role of the executive. . . ." There should, in fact, be a mutual commitment by the governor and the legislature to build up one another's institutions, not to tear them down. In some states the office of governor may need strengthening as much or more than the legislature itself. Curiously then, it is to the legislature's advantage, as well as to the state's, for gubernatorial power within the executive to be enhanced. As they improve their own branch, legislators should and can also improve the executive. They have done so in Wisconsin, where the legislature enacted a major bill reducing some eighty-seven executive agencies into thirteen departments and a few related boards. They have done so in Florida, where the legislature passed a reorganization act granting the governor significantly more control over a fragmented executive.

One important reason for legislatures to attend closely to the executive branch is that governors and legislators, as politicians elected to represent the people, have similar stakes in controlling professionals in the administrative departments and agencies of state government. Too often, the professional bureaucracies are responsive neither to the governor nor to the legislature. Yet both the governor and the legislature share the responsibility for establishing policy and making sure that it is implemented efficiently and effectively. For the governor, a major means of control is the executive budgetary process. Through the budget, and his review of department and agency requests for funds, the governor can ensure that his priorities are reflected in the conduct of government and can exercise control over the administrative establishment.

The legislature's role in overseeing the executive branch, which has traditionally been referred to as "legislative oversight," should be of great significance. In the past, however, legislative review and evaluation of administration and the effects of state policies and programs has been woefully neglected. This neglect can be attributed to the fact that legislators have been so absorbed in the process of decision-making that they have had little opportunity to explore the consequences of decisions they have made. Add to this the lack of work during interim periods, the disabilities of standing committees, and the inadequacy of investigative and evaluative resources, and the legislature's oversight of "legislative oversight" becomes quite understandable.

Review and evaluation of programs and administration will become a major task for state legislatures in the years ahead. An initial effort is under way. Program budgeting is gradually being developed, and accomplishment in program and performance auditing is not many years away. California, Colorado, Florida, Hawaii, Oregon, and Wisconsin are moving deliberately forward. Other states will undoubtedly be following their examples. The Connecticut General Assembly and the Eagleton Institute are participating jointly in a three-year demonstration project to devise an effective system of legislative review and evaluation. Opportunities for the more rational consideration of state programs and the improved performance of state administration are at hand. To make the most of them, legislatures will simply have to work harder, redirect the efforts of members and committees, and dedicate their energies to unglamorous but nonetheless critical tasks.

V

The views of executive and legislative leaders are consonant with regard to the general steps state legislatures must take if they are to strengthen themselves, become more responsible, and increase their competence. Can all or much of this be done? Robert P. Knowles—president pro tem and formerly majority leader of the Wisconsin Senate and past president of the National Conference of State Legislative Leaders—considers the prospects. In his essay, which concludes Part Two of this volume, he describes the broad thrust of legislative improvement and then discusses just how it can be achieved. On the basis of long experience promoting the cause of legislative reform throughout the nation, he notes that although the pace may be slow, the resources are available. Relevant information exists, and support from national organizations and state citizen groups can be enlisted. But the primary responsibility for institutional improvement resides with the legislature itself. More than anything else, Mr. Knowles believes, "the inspiration for modernization must come from within the legislature. . . . it cannot be imposed from the outside." Then, and only then, will the demands and proposals for more effective legislatures be translated into reality.

From the Governor's Chair . . .

HAROLD E. HUGHES

Everybody recognizes the power of the Congress. Few citizens understand the powers of a state legislature or how it exerts those powers. Figuratively (and sometimes literally), the state legislature has been the sleeper in our federal system. It is generally agreed by professionals in government that our state legislatures are in urgent need of upgrading. There is substantial agreement on what needs to be done to modernize and improve the legislative function. But getting the job done in the face of public apathy and distaste for reform is something else. It is necessary to keep the dialogue going, the pressure constantly applied.

With regard to the uneasy matrimony that exists between a governor and his state legislature, I do not consider myself an authority, but I have at least had a variety of experience. I served as governor of Iowa for three terms, dealing with three sessions of our biennial legislature. In the first of these sessions, there was a Republican majority in both houses of the General Assembly. In the second session, there was a Democratic majority in both houses—something that happens in Iowa only about once in thirty years. In the third session, there was a Republican House and a narrow Democratic majority in the Senate.

I can testify that the maintenance of a constructive relationship between governor and legislature under any of these circumstances is not easy. The assumption that a chief executive is assured of success with his legislative program by having a large majority of his own party in both houses of the state legislature is not borne out by the history of my state, where frequently we have had a Republican governor with overwhelming Republican majorities in both houses—and a clean sweep of the elective state offices, as well.

The apartheid between the governor and the legislature is deeper than party differences. Most chief executives are convinced that the vast majority of legislators do not understand the problems of the executive. Legislators are equally certain that the old man simply does not understand the legislative process. To a large extent they are both right. Beyond a doubt, there is substantial room for improvement in the typical relationship between a chief executive and his state's legislature. Yet this is a subtle matter that does not particularly lend itself to the direct approach. The governor and the lawmakers should respect one another and understand one another's prerogatives better than they do, but if the proper separation of powers is to be preserved, they should not be too fraternal.

As general legislative reforms, such as annual sessions, compensation, expenses, staff, office space, and research assistance are put into effect, I believe that benefits to the relationship between the legislature and the executive will accrue. Take annual sessions, which is one of several constitutional amendments for reorganization of the legislature that I proposed and supported as governor in Iowa. Understanding and cooperation between executive and legislative branches should be strengthened by annual sessions, if only because the two branches will be forced into a closer togetherness.

It is not generally understood by the average citizen that our legislatures have traditionally governed not so much by legislating as by *not* legislating. Bills that are extraordinarily bad and regressive are generally derailed before they get through the entire legislative process. But more significant is the fact that good and important bills are stifled in committees or permitted to languish on legislative calendars. By the simple stratagem of not legislating on vital public interest issues, a state legislature can effectively preserve the status quo and keep a state in the oxcart era. And this, of course, is the way that the lawmakers can give the governor his comeuppance.

With the legislature in session every year, I think the public will demand more constructive action and will be less indifferent to failures in the legislative process. It has been my experience with the biennial legislative format that the people complain bitterly about the shortcomings of the legislature while it is in session, but then promptly forget about it during the interim period, as women are said to forget about the pain of childbirth. Annual sessions will eliminate this happy amnesia.

It is also my belief that the growing adaptation of modern technology and planning techniques to the massive problems of state government will be of benefit to both executive and legislative branches and facilitate their interworking.

Much of the organizational reform in state government that we have seen in America in recent years has been directed toward shoring up the powers of our "weak" governors and pinpointing their responsibilities. In Iowa, we had mixed results along these lines during my terms as governor. For example, we passed a constitutional amendment for an item veto in appropriations bills, but failed to make the governor's cabinet appointive or to adopt four-year terms with governor and lieutenant governor running as a team. The organizational changes in the role of the governor in relation to the legislature have been constructive and long needed. But I am convinced that we need to change our fundamental attitudes and concepts, as well. Reorganization, however sound and thoroughgoing it may be, cannot do the job alone.

Governors, under our weak-governor system, have sometimes been weaker than the system required them to be, for the simple reason that they were unwilling to put their prestige on the line for public-interest goals—particularly in legislative matters. Legislators are prone to take a parochial view of their role. They operate in the arena of the two chambers and the committee rooms. These settings are remote from the vast, far-flung departments of state government and from the public. There is not much awareness on the part of either the executive or the legislative branches that they are both integral parts of the same state government.

On their attitudes toward their political subdivisions—particularly the cities—both governors and legislatures are apt to share the belief that these subdivisions are errant stepchildren whose needs are properly relegated to a second echelon of priorities. The chief executive and the legislature are also likely to share the same attitude toward the federal government: that it is an alien and essentially hostile power. In many cases, both governor and legislature are more hindrance than help in the middle-man spot they occupy between federal grants-in-aid programs and local jurisdictions.

Another base of agreement between governors and legislatures is on states' rights and prerogatives. They both complain loudly about the erosion of states' rights, without really demonstrating either the imagination or initiative to do anything to strengthen the state's role. No governmental subject has been more widely discussed in recent years than the decline of the influence of the state in our federal system. The frustration with the diminishing role of the state and the resentment over the growing incursion of the federal government into areas that should more logically belong to the state, dominated the agenda at the national governors' conferences in all the years I attended them. In fact, at times it seemed to me as if this was the *only* subject that they were willing to talk about. Obviously there was too much preoccupation with states' rights and too little attention to the state government's obligations and responsibilities.

If state government is to become the vital cog in our federal system that it should be, then those who represent the states—in both legislative and executive branches—must work for this objective and fight for it to an extent undreamed of in the past. The governors and state legislatures need to form a more cohesive team, not just in working relationships but in basic attitudes about our federal-state-local system of shared responsibility.

Bluntly speaking, there hasn't been a greater "never the twain shall meet" precedent anywhere in our public life than between stubborn chief executives and militant state legislatures. A unity of purpose on basic goals is needed. It is time for governors and state legislators, on the one hand, and the mayors of the cities, on the other, to quit throwing brickbats at one another from behind their traditional barricades. We have some fundamental business at hand that we must transact together—namely, the preservation of our union. And the union, quite plainly, is the people, not the jurisdictions of government.

I believe we need new and constructive dialogue between the branches of government and between the levels of government. We need to listen, give ground, eat crow, negotiate, conciliate, and do whatever is necessary to preserve our federal system. In politics, as elsewhere, the scriptural admonition applies: "Pride goeth before destruction, and a haughty spirit before a fall."

During my years as governor, I frankly was not enchanted by all the aid programs that came out of Washington, nor was I always happy about the way they were administered. By and large, the legislature could be counted on to be hostile toward anything that came from Washington. This is a typical situation in most states. But it is important for governors and legislators to recognize that these programs have pumped lifeblood into local areas in such fields as education, hospitals, public works, urban renewal, recreation facilities, and so on down the line. In short, they have helped people at the grass roots, in ways desperately needed.

It is not the proper function of the state, as I see it, to throw up roadblocks to the administration of these programs, but rather to provide constructive assistance at both ends so that the work will progress in an orderly manner with the least possible confusion, duplication of effort, and delay. Legislators and governors should cooperate to this end. If a federal program of aid to local government is not functioning properly, then I construe it to be the state government's job to shake up the administrators in Washington by whatever means required.

Similarly, the state government should *serve* local government, as well as regulate it, on matters within the state. I feel that it should *represent* and *champion* local government units in their transactions with the federal government. This is a responsibility that both governors and legislators should acknowledge and shoulder, and, in all candor, most of them have not done this.

The state, through its governor and its legislature, should also take a more active role in stating what is needed at state and local levels, instead of waiting for the initiative to come from Washington. Neither governors nor legislatures have any notable resemblance to Santa Claus when it comes to sharing state revenues with local jurisdictions, particularly cities and towns. Although it is true that state governments are strapped for revenues, the city governments are in even more desperate straits.

In my opinion, state governments should extend policies of revenue sharing with local governments, even if the dimension of the aid is comparatively small. The concept of the state being concerned about its political subdivisions is essential to the strengthening of our federal system. Although both governor and legislature should take heed of this point, it is generally the legislature that wins the blue ribbon for obliviousness to local governments' financial needs.

The relationship between the state's chief executive and its legislature is a key area in our federal system—and one where there is unquestionably room for improvement. As I suggested earlier, I am convinced that revision of our attitudes may be even more important than reorganization of our governmental machinery in this connection. In the final reckoning, we are not looking for a "strong-governor system" or a "weak-governor system," but for a dynamic and responsive state government that is strong in all branches and in its over-all, coordinated operation.

From the Governor's Chair . . .

RICHARD B. OGILVIE

Understanding the relationship between a governor and a legislature comes from a clearer recognition of the role of each within the broader political system of that state. The governor's role with regard to the legislature has been characterized in Clinton Rossiter's phrase as "chief legislator." But what does that mean? Does it mean that the governor is a broad policy advocate, a spokesman for people, proponent of public causes and conscience for public needs? Or does it mean he is a major participant in the arena of compromise, a conciliator with sleeves rolled up at the bargaining table? Probably in the real world it means some of both, but the questions for each governor are which role should be played and which role is he permitted to play within the political environment of his state.

On the legislative side of the picture, there has been great interest in recent years in the revitalization of the legislature as an institution and as an instrument to shape public policy. There have been numerous state study commissions and reports, and various national organizations have made significant commitments of money and resources in order to develop the legislature as a strong and independent branch of government.

Redressing the imbalance in the role of the legislature is a task that the states have faced much more adequately than has the U. S. Congress. The states have demonstrated their leadership in coming to grips with one of the fundamental problems in American democracy's doctrine of separation of powers. The contrast of state efforts to the halting and futile efforts to reform congressional operations reaffirms the vitality of another fundamental principle of American democracy: federalism, where innovation and change can come from either level of government.

In many states legislatures have made great strides to develop the necessary tools of streamlined procedures, adequate compensation, improved physical facilities, and trained professional staffs. But in many cases these changes have not produced any demonstrable improvement in the legislative work product. Judged in terms of results, in many instances these tools, beneficial in themselves, have not adequately solved the problem of legislative unresponsiveness to public demands.

Perhaps it is appropriate and timely for a broader look at the role of both the individual legislator and of the legislature within the context of the general political framework and system of the state. Despite its new trappings, I believe that each legislature today faces an identity crisis of its own.

One of the major thrusts of legislative reform is to develop the ability of a legislature as the elected representative of the people to innovate, originate, conceptualize, and specifically formulate changes in public policy by statutory action and through the allocation of public resources. It has been said repeatedly that the legislature must do more than act like a traffic court judge, merely voting up or down a governor's program and special-interest bills.

I have observed two significant roadblocks to this kind of "strong legislature" model. Both relate to the way the legislator views his role. These roadblocks are not impediments imposed by chief executives, trying to centralize power or subjugate a legislature; for I believe most governors would welcome a strong legislature, if the members recognized their responsibilities as well as their authority. Impediments to legislative reform today are centered not in public apathy or executive jealousy but in the attitudes within the legislative branch itself.

The first roadblock concerns the threshold question of how a legislator sees his own role. How does a legislator view prospective votes on issues? Do these constitute opportunities or burdens? Does he approach a decision with the expectation of gaining public support or with the fear of voter reprisal? Do votes on issues help or are they negative? These kinds of questions many will answer with: "Oh, it depends on the issue." But that is not so—it depends more on a state of mind! No matter how unpopular or unpleasant a political issue, if a legislator believes in his decision, then he can present it positively to the voters. There are many he will not convert on the issue, but he can gain the respect and support of many more citizens by candor, frankness, sincerity, reasonableness, and commitment. But many legislators, and some governors, view votes or decisions as negatives, to be feared because somebody is not going to like them, rather than as opportunities for developing public confidence and understanding. These negative legislators believe that the best possible session is one in which there is no need to cast any votes.

Similarly, many legislators do not feel a responsibility to seek out problem areas of public concern and to search for solutions. They view their job as primarily that of a judge, reviewing the case or controversy before them, relying on the adversary proceeding of hearings and debate, and rendering a verdict by their votes.

Both those who avoid most issues because of their potential negative voter impact and those who see a passive judicial role as appropriate will, by their legislative actions, prevent institutional reforms in the legislature from affecting the work product. In reality they are satisfied with the work product of a legislature that defers resolution of controversial proposals or innovative solutions to another place—presumably the executive branch. Until these legislators see their responsibility to their constituents as an active one, legislative reform will be for naught.

The second, and perhaps most significant, roadblock to a "strong legislature" is the legislature's role within the partisan political environment of the state. This environment varies greatly among the states, but it is crucial to the real role a legislature can play. Institutional factors in the political system of the state may severely restrict or limit the actual operations of the legislature. We talk of an "independent legislature," and we usually think of legislative independence in relationship to the governor and the executive branch. But is the concept of legislative independence in accord with political reality?

The legislature historically has been the melting pot or the arena for compromise—the institution where diverse interests and objectives and different perspectives come together and where some concept of action is achieved. The legislature works within a standard set of rules for the resolution of conflict. It is considered so important as the true representative of the public will that the courts, as the final authority in our systems of law enforcement, are required to defer to the expressed legislative statement and intent, even when the result in a given case is seen as the product of erroneous or even malicious legislative deliberations.

The legislature on its own operates in its labyrinthian and often mysterious ways through committees, commissions, leadership, individual members, and party caucuses, all of which are devices to institutionalize practices and methods to arrive at compromises for conflicting values and to develop common grounds for concerted action.

The over-all political system in a state may not view the legislature in that state as the proper forum for the resolution of conflicting political objectives. For example, it may regard the legislature as only a small part of a broader political contest between a few major individuals as party leaders. This obviously means that the legislature in such states is not going to be generally innovative in originating solutions. The realities of the political framework of the state do not place the legislature in that role. Take my own state as an example. The Democratic party of Cook County is a very efficient and effective political organization. It operates large portions of the governmental machinery on both the state and local levels. Its strength injects a very different factor into our legislature. With some few exceptions, nearly all of its members of the Illinois General Assembly recognize by their own choice that their first loyalty is to the organization, not to themselves or their own district constituencies. They will vote without hesitation, for example, for a party reapportionment plan that eliminates their own seat, because as individuals they will be accommodated somewhere else in the system by the party in elective or appointive office.

I am not finding fault, or saying that they are poorer legislators or that they are not good men of good will. But I am saying that they have chosen voluntarily to submit to a rigid party discipline on the theory that they will achieve their own interests and ambitions by this "team" attitude, by a central determination of public interest, and with no variance by the different component constituencies they represent. What is important is how this large voting bloc of tightly disciplined members affects a legislative body.

The Democratic party Cook County organization, I believe, sees the political environment of Illinois as one where the leaders of the political parties are the focal point for the resolution of conflict—a summit conference theory drawn from the parallel experience in foreign policy. This role sees the legislature like the United Nations, important for fixing an image and for setting the scene, but not as the institution or the arena for real conflict resolution.

As an added follow-up to my example, I must point out that the "summit theory" strategy of one political party and the theory of the other party that the legislature is a representative forum have often caused real tension and an inadequate political decision-making system as far as the public is concerned. In this critique I am not making judgments, but rather striving to be clinical. The Republican party as it is constituted in Illinois consists of a wide variety of independently elected local leaders. It simply will not and cannot accept rigid party leadership in any disciplined manner. Consequently each party is unable to use the other's methods or system, and this poses a fundamental problem not only for viewing the role of the legislature but also for the viability of the political system of the state.

Obviously a governor in relating to a legislature is going to have very different strategies, depending on different political systems and different situations. If the legislature is dominated by men afraid to face issues squarely, by men who seek the "agreed bill" compromise process on every issue, then the governor must become a strong advocate. He must push for progress and become a spokesman for change. That is, of course, if you accept the premise, as I do, that state governments must do a great deal more to solve the problems of our people. If, on the other hand, the political system allocates a secondary role to the legislature as such, then a governor must develop his role as party leader and spokesman. That may mean frequent recognition of legislators as important elected political leaders from various areas, who can be helpful in consultation and development of positions before they are taken and loyal team members once decisions are reached.

If neither of these major impediments stands in the way of a strong legislature, then a third, more classical view of the governor's role should be taken. The governor must be a proposer and compromiser. He must assume his statewide role with a careful eye to his broad constituency, while the individual legislator has a narrower base. But the governor must work with the legislature as a partner; the individual legislator must recognize his role as a part of a collective body; and the legislative body must be respected as the agent of compromise and the arena of change. The governor and his executive departments must work with each part of the legislature—its committees, its individual members, and its party leadership. Their joint efforts to develop solutions and their early consultations on major decisions are essential to the system. But it is a two-way process.

The governor is elected by the people, and is presumed to bring to the office public support for his general positions on public issues. And so are legislators. Yet, as time goes on, a great divergence often appears in the relationship between governor and legislators. I have tried to understand why. One reason is that the governor faces not only legislative issues, but the great portion of his time is spent as chief executive, operating the government from day to day. He must make decisions on a vast array of issues about implementing broad policies and managing a major corporate enterprise. Legislators often become so absorbed in the process of decision-making that they have little touch with the realities of the results of the decisions they make.

If the legislature wants to be a real partner in the conduct of the government, then the legislators must take the time and the effort to become informed and to see the world as it is. How many legislators have visited even one of the state prisons or mental hospitals or universities for other than a football game? How many have seen a public assistance office, much less some welfare recipients' homes? How many have talked with teachers and principals and students at local schools about real education issues?

Those are things their partners in the executive branch are doing each day. Legislators cannot and should not be expected to see things as administrators do or to know all the details of government operations. But they ought to be far better informed and more aware of what executives are coping with in administering state policies and programs. They will not get information or awareness by mere cross-examination in an ornate capitol building hearing room or from speeches by other politicians in legislative chambers.

Governors will welcome legislatures as partners. But legislatures must be willing to bear some responsibility—both actual and moral. Then the legislature can assume its rightful role as an independent and innovative branch of government. Then the reforms, the improvements, and the new tools will be meaningful to the final legislative product, and then the public will benefit greatly from a responsive political system. Legislative and executive partners can restore the faith of the people in the idea that change is possible and that the public interest is represented—in short, in the belief that democracy works.

From the Governor's Chair . . .

CARL E. SANDERS

As a member of the Georgia General Assembly for eight years and as a governor who worked closely, harmoniously, and productively with the distinguished members of the Georgia General Assembly, I am in complete sympathy and agreement with the goal of bringing improvement to state legislatures.

The details may differ from state to state, but the broad thrust is universal. We need smaller, more professional legislative bodies. We need legislators who devote more time to the job, who are better paid, and who have longer terms in which to learn their job; we need longer sessions and better rules of procedures to make the most of the time available to the legislature. We need stronger committees that develop real expertise in their areas of responsibility. We desperately need qualified research staffs and clerical assistance. To do an adequate job, the legislatures must have adequate space and facilities. It is clear that before many years go by, almost every legislature in the land must have its own computerized data processing system.

But why do we need these things? Why must state legislative bodies change their traditional methods of doing business?

Some ninety-five years ago, the respresentative from Banks

County, Georgia, James Jackson Turnbull, rode his horse to the nearest railroad station and got on a chugging, coal-fired train to Atlanta to attend the General Assembly. On February 14, 1875, he wrote his wife, Mary, as follows: "I hope it will not be many days til we adjourn. The 40 days will expire next Monday week, the 22nd instant. It is generally believed, though, the session will be extended. Over 700 bills have been introduced and only about 30 disposed of. It would seem from this showing *that we are getting on slowly.*" State legislatures are still *getting on slowly*—almost a century later. Except that today, instead of having seven hundred bills to consider, the Georgia General Assembly can expect over two thousand.

The real problem is not one of sheer numbers. Instead, the difficulty lies in the complexity and interrelationships of today's problems, with which the flood of bills attempts to deal. We are faced with an information explosion of staggering dimensions and, so far at least, have taken only limited steps to contain it. The magnitude of our problems has become apparent only within the past decade. I can use the experience of my own state of Georgia to illustrate some major advances and some roadblocks as well.

Since one of the most controversial areas of state government today is the financial area, let me use Georgia's budgeting process as an illustrative example of the problem facing state government today. In 1942, the total of state spending was under fifty million dollars. By 1963, the first year that Georgia's legislature was presented with a comprehensive state budget, spending had risen to almost 450 million dollars. The governor's proposed budget for fiscal 1970 went over the billion-dollar mark for the first time.

Nine years ago, when I was president pro tem of the state Senate, we enacted a law creating Georgia's first professionally staffed budget bureau. For the previous thirty years the effective control of Georgia's public funds had been in the hands of one man, the state auditor. He had that power, because in the 1930s the Georgia General Assembly had spurned his attempts to present it with a budget. The legislature simply could not be bothered with that much information about state government. In 1962, we wrote a new budget act creating a professional budget bureau under the governor and allowing the General Assembly to employ its own budget analyst. Today, we have a top-notch budget bureau, developed under the leadership of a former legislator. But the legislature has yet to hire the budget analyst it promised itself *nine years ago*.

In 1968, the Georgia General Assembly for the first time in seven years seriously challenged a governor's budget. The House appropriations committee held extensive hearings. The almost sixty members of the committee sat day after day listening to department pleas for funds; but when the time came to cut the budget, the committee had to turn to the state auditor for suggestions as to what could be trimmed. The committee was neither organized nor staffed to receive the necessary budget information and act on it.

The lesson is clear. The executive branch has moved ahead to try to cope with the times; the legislative branch has talked a good game, but somehow has not managed to keep up. This is a tragedy for state government. It is particularly a tragedy because most state governments are much more in the hands of their legislatures than they are in the hands of their governors. A strong, progressive, modern state government requires a strong, progressive, modern state legislature. In years of billion-dollar budgets, state legislatures are responding almost as they did in years of fifty-million-dollar budgets.

The delayed response by legislatures is not all the fault of the legislators themselves; perhaps it is not even principally their fault. For years able, dedicated state legislative leaders have pleaded for improvements. But state legislatures are caught in a vicious circle. Too often in the past they have been concerned only with the petty and the trivial. It has been too easy for journalists, and scholars as well, to hold up foolish legislative action to scorn and ridicule. Legislatures have not organized themselves to ask the tough questions, the right questions about priorities in these demanding times. They have not demanded that the executive branch concern itself about priorities. They have not insisted on accurate, long-range information about where state government is going. Too many voters for too long a time have not perceived state legislative seats as positions of importance, and consequently have been willing to send men of little stature to occupy them.

But a mood of change is in the air. There are evident signs that the public is beginning to wake up to the necessity of supporting its state legislative bodies in their attempts to strengthen their role in state government. The Citizens Conference on State Legislatures has sparked citizen support for legislative improvement in state after state. I have watched with interest the work of the Citizens Committee on the Georgia General Assembly. Its distinguished members, sponsored by the Citizens Conference and assisted by able research staff from the university system, are in the process of making public recommendations for specific improvements for the Georgia General Assembly.

The Citizens Committee in Georgia has been completely independent of the legislature, even raising its own funds. But it has had the support of Speaker George Smith and Lieutenant Governor George T. Smith. Because of its independence this committee can point with equal clarity to faults and strong points. It can criticize the General Assembly, and it can criticize the public for its nonsupport of much-needed reforms.

To give our state legislatures their proper place in a progressive state government, we have to have able, dedicated representatives with the staff and facilities to enable them to do an adequate job. To get that kind of men and women for legislative office, we have to provide them with much higher salaries and accord them much more status. Yet status, respect, and even high salaries must be earned; they will not fall from heaven simply because it would be nice to have them. Before the public is going to go along with buying admittedly expensive improvements, it is going to have to be convinced that state legislatures are doing a top-notch job with what they already have.

Objective public opinion polls show that the average citizen has little respect for most public officials, including members of state legislatures. If that climate of opinion is to be altered, the public must be made aware of the strong points of our legislative bodies. It should know about the long hours and tedious study put in by dedicated legislators. It should know about such things as the Georgia freshman legislators' study seminars, conducted at their own expense. It should know that most legislators, compared to other professional occupations, are overworked, underpaid, and provided with miserable working conditions.

But it requires time and effort to spread good news; and it requires much more good news to overshadow the occasional examples of poor conduct that do occur.

From the Governor's Chair . . .

WARREN P. KNOWLES

A governor does not often have the chance to express openly his views on the legislature and his relationship to it. It is a most appealing opportunity. In my thirty years of public service, I have been on both sides of the fence. I started out as a member of the board of supervisors in my home county in Wisconsin, then spent fourteen years as a state senator, followed by six years as lieutenant governor, and finally six years as governor. As I look back on those years, I become more and more convinced that the wisely conceived checks and balances inherent in our separation of powers have made it possible for Wisconsin to be recognized as a progressive state, which effectively solves problems, institutes reforms, and provides leadership on statewide matters that affect all of the people.

Wisconsin's record of achievement, however, has not been free of conflict among the three branches of government. Many times the executive has felt that the legislature was attempting to step beyond its proper role, and vice versa; and sometimes the executive and the legislature have been united in wondering just what the judiciary was up to.

What are the proper roles? In practice, it is hard to say. Gray areas cause concern, but as the chief executive of Wisconsin, I try very hard to operate within this basic framework. The legislature is the board of directors—the policy makers and the reviewers of the policy they set. Quite separate and distinct is the executive—the chairman or adviser of the board and president or operating manager of the programs established to carry out the policies of the board. Just as the board members usually are selected to represent specific interests, so are legislators. Just as the president is expected to represent the entire spectrum of interests, so is the state government executive. There is also the judiciary, whose job it is to resolve conflicts and interpret the laws resulting from the policies established by the legislature.

We are all aware of the nationwide attempts to strengthen state legislatures. I fully support the concept. A stronger legislature will have the capability to spell out sounder policies, and more effective programs to administer those policies should naturally result. But two things concern me as the need to strengthen legislatures gathers momentum. One, which is talked about much, is the absolute necessity for more staff. Staff may be needed, but a revitalized legislature will not result from a full staff complement, accompanied by a continued reluctance to change policies or to adopt new ones simply because present policies do not rock the boat at election time. Staff assistance is not a substitute for hard work. A legislator willing to work hard and to rely on staff assistance in developing solutions to new problems in state government is the one who could use a staff. Many legislators do not overexert themselves, nor do many legislative bodies. More staff is not a panacea for the frustrations of legislatures.

The other disturbing feature of discussions about strengthening legislatures is the implication by some that the best way to achieve a stronger legislature is to weaken the executive branch. If this approach is taken literally, what is the result? A legislature that has not changed is a weak and ineffective administrator of its policies. A similar approach would be to add powers and authorities to the legislature and take them away from the executive. This would create a situation where programs—urgent and necessary programs vital to the state—would be operated by as many legislators as there are districts and by as many viewpoints as there are special interests. In short, state government would not function. It might have grand policies, but it would not operate.

The legislature has fundamental responsibilities and powers granted by basic charter. It need not, it cannot perform the management function. It is the executive, and not individual legislators, who is elected by *all of the people* to provide direction and administer programs *for all of the people*. The obvious course is to strengthen and improve the legislature and the executive—not one at the expense of the other, but simultaneously—so that they may strive toward mutual goals of good government, which parenthetically is also good politics.

I am a firm believer in the legislative process, and I agree that it needs modernizing. The process where all views are considered and are mixed together with the realities of state problems to form workable legislation is a sound one and is basic to our democracy. However, after the package is presented to the chief executive it must be his responsibility and duty as the choice of the majority of *all* the people to make sure the legislation is administered for the benefit of *everyone*. Special interests and the active participation of pressure groups and lobbyists dictate that the people be represented by one who can review legislation as to its effect on public policy and assess the fiscal implications. It must be the executive's responsibility and duty, and his alone. This separation of power and authority need not lead to divisiveness in the state house.

There is nothing to prevent the executive from sitting down with legislators to define a problem and come up with a good approach toward solving it. Not enough of this has been done. The legislature should not have any fear of dealing with the chief executive. I have none, and I welcome direct head-to-head communication with the legislature.

It is not easy sometimes to consult and work with the legislature, including legislative leaders of one's own party. One of the problems is the lack of time. In preparing a legislative program, a budget, or a revenue measure, my staff and members of the department of administration have had to work day and night, seven days a week, before the legislature convenes and even when the legislature is in session. Yet, if we announce the program without consulting legislators, they are disturbed. If we consult with them ahead of time, the story leaks and we are criticized, even before the program is publicly announced. What is worse, our own leaders, because of their disagreement, prevent us from presenting an agreed-upon program. As a result, I feel very strongly today that the chief executive must present the administration program as he sees it and then let the legislature act accordingly.

Another problem is that legislators themselves feel that they should present their own program. The question that arises is: Who represents the party in power—the governor, the legislature, or a combination of both? Speaking politically, it would seem to me that the executive, with some consultation with legislative leaders, especially of his own party, should present the administration's program; and the legislative leaders, through consultation with the chief executive, should eventually come around to support the administration's legislative program.

We have had several other problems with legislators in the area of appointments and the scheduling of the governor's time. Some legislators have felt that they should be consulted on every appointment made. This, of course, is impossible, although we make every attempt to consult with legislators from the area in which an appointment may be made. We have known some legislators to recommend several different people for the same job. If they only appreciated the headaches and the problems involved in conscientiously making appointments to commissions, boards, and so forth, I am sure they would be happy to have someone else do the job.

The other problem is that of finding time to meet with legislators in my office and having legislators invite me to meet with constituents in their local areas. Legislators often drop in the office unannounced and without previous appointment, but insistent on seeing the governor. As you know, governors are generally busy every minute of the day, but meeting legislators is a high priority in my office. We have solved this problem by having my secretary escort me from my office into the legislator's when he wishes to see me, even though I may have a previous commitment. And, of course, we try to meet the requests of legislators for my presence in their counties. This, again, may be most difficult, but they view appearances in their county, no matter how small or how few people will be on hand, as far more important than any appearance elsewhere.

These may seem like minor problems. But one legislator has actually told my secretary that "If the governor will appear in my town on Dairy Day, I will vote for his bill." Another legislator, who could not see me when he appeared in my office unexpectedly and without an appointment, vowed never again to visit the governor. I simply mention these factors because they are practical, everyday occurrences, which can influence the success of legislation.

One comment about the legislative process itself is also in order. It refers to something that greatly concerns me. I think that I have a good understanding of politics, thirty years of understanding. But there are times in the legislative process when politics—partisan politics—gives the entire legislature a black eye in the minds of the public. Does it do any good at all to inject partisanship in the legislative process simply to be obstinate? Does it do any good at all to play brinksmanship with the majority party—to play the "outpromise" game—at the expense of a solution?

The important goal is not just a stronger legislature, the goal is better state government. My own view is that the best politics is good government, and conversely good government will benefit politicians of both political parties who do a creditable job and who will gain personal satisfaction.

From the Leader's Position . . .

CHARLES F. KURFESS

Today, it is virtually impossible for state legislators to be unaware of the discussion and consideration being given by many, in and out of government, to our federal structure and the relationships and responsibilities of the several layers of government. Now is a most appropriate time to consider the so-called "new federalism" and attempt to direct to state government new and greater responsibilities, and to redirect some responsibilities the states may well have forfeited in the past by inaction or conscious avoidance. Although the situations vary considerably from state to state, the challenges and opportunities faced by state government today are more complex and more far-reaching than the problems of the past, and state legislatures have, therefore, more cause than ever to attempt to strengthen their hands in order to deal with them.

What a legislature should be may well vary considerably from state to state, depending on a number of factors: constitutional, social, economic, historical, political, and so forth. However, I think it is most important that each legislature be in a position to determine the role it is to assume. And if legislators are in fact going to be able to assume a determining role in their own destinies, they are going to have to analyze not only the present status of their legislatures, but also the means or lack of means available for them to determine their future role.

First, we must consider how legislators individually, and thereby as a legislative body, view their job. How do they perceive their role and their sometimes conflicting responsibilities? If we are to fulfill our roles most responsibly and effectively, we must do much more than merely reflect the attitudes of constituents at a particular time when specific matters are before the legislature. A legislator's decisions must many times be primarily those of a "state" representative, perhaps modified in part by considerations of his own particular district. These broader interests and broader concerns cannot be based on a "you scratch my back and I'll scratch yours" philosophy of yesteryear. They should reflect the increasing interest and concern not only of those with governmental responsibility, but the interest and concern of one's own constituents for statewide problems as well as a member's own awareness that the problems of one segment of our society will inevitably be felt by other segments. Improved communication and population mobility have made it impractical for an effective legislator to focus narrowly on his own district while ignoring the rest of the state.

As our society and economy have grown more complex, government has continually assumed a greater involvement in the lives of people and business. To fulfill their most useful function, however, legislators must be in a position to anticipate conditions and not merely react to them. They will then be able to represent the true interests of their constituents and their future. And, of course, legislators will always do a better job by anticipating and meeting situations before they reach a state of urgency and before alternative forms of action are precluded by crisis developments. Hasty judgments made during such circumstances can overlook complicated ramifications, ones that might be perceived if there were greater review and deliberation.

To be effective in the task of problem-solving and problem-avoiding, and still maintain that very essential relationship with constituents, legislators will obviously need to be in good communication with those they are to represent. They must have the means to apprise people of the concerns and potential situations that are faced, the alternative solutions and courses of action available, and the reasons one course is selected over others.

In other words, legislators must not only attempt to represent the viewpoint of their constituents and what is best for their future, but must also keep them informed, since the public is perhaps not initially aware of and knowledgeable concerning the ramifications of the actions taken and those rejected. The effective legislature will often find itself not only enacting a program, but also having to sell it.

If legislatures are to assume and fulfill effectively such a vital and responsible role, they will also need to have the organizational structure and procedures that provide an adequate form for deliberations, that encourage legislative involvement in policy making, and that help to carry out legislative intent. In this regard probably every legislature, regardless of past reforms, would benefit by examining many facets of its structure, practices, and procedures.

Are the numbers of legislators sufficient to assure a constituency that it can know its legislator, but still not too many for the legislative bodies to be effectively organized with full participation by the members? Is prefiling of bills provided so legislative work can be undertaken expeditiously at the beginning of a session? Are there means, such as deadlines for the filing of bills, to keep the session from dragging on ad infinitum and to minimize the usual hectic wrapup in a legislative session? Do committees proliferate in order to provide numerous chairmanships, or are they organized so that each committee is assigned a substantial area of responsibility in which it can act? Are committees bogged down with ineffective chairmen who attain and keep their positions by virture of seniority alone? Do the public and interested parties have the opportunity of being heard by legislative committees? Are legislative committees structured and staffed to provide a degree of legislative oversight of administrative departments and undertakings? Is a legislative record, especially of committee deliberations, adequately maintained and published, to make clear to the administrators and to the courts exactly what the legislative intent was with regard to an enacted measure? Are there restrictions, legal or practical, upon the length of sessions that hamper the legislative endeavor?

Another matter to be considered in many of our states is annual sessions versus biennial sessions, and here again, the legislature itself should have a great degree of control over its own work schedule. Our own recent experience in Ohio has indicated that with annual sessions, adjustments have to be made in procedures to accommodate the change from biennial meetings with special sessions. The major advantages of annual sessions are that they give the legislature the wherewithal to pay much closer attention to its fiscal responsibilities, even without going to an annual budget, and also provide for much greater and thorough committee study and action in areas of concern that cannot adequately be dealt with in a typical annual session.

In working with budgets, legislatures must assume the full responsibility that goes with their being the primary revenue-raising and appropriating agency of state government. When one has the responsibility of raising revenues from naturally reluctant taxpayers, one must also assume the responsibility of stewardship by applying these funds to the best interests of the people and their needs. Legislative bodies should be thoroughly informed through their budget hearings and staff procedures to be able to anticipate clearly the specific application of those funds, and to be able to review that application at the next budget hearing to determine if legislative intent is being met. In this area, legislatures must be prepared to evaluate the benefits that programs achieve in relation to their costs.

Many legislatures in the past have been far too dependent

on staffs of administrative departments and special-interest organizations for their basic information. It is not necessary that the legislature duplicate these staffs either in number or in expertise, but it *is* essential that competent staff personnel be available to assist in analyzing the presentations made by the departments and by private representatives.

Consideration of administrative programs ought to include examination of alternatives, and these can often be discovered only by the legislature's own inquiry. The legislative staff should make it possible for the legislature to take the initiative, not only in deciding a direction or course of action, but also in determining what areas and problems to attack. At the same time, when specialized expertise is needed for extended study projects or complicated measures, the legislature should have the means to retain its own consultants. To be most effective, it is also necessary that legislators know how to use such staff and their work without subverting their own role as elected representatives in favor of the so-called "ivory tower boys." Staff should also be available to assist in answering inquiries of legislators and doing the legwork they are often called upon to perform on behalf of constituents in their dealings with government.

To function effectively, adequate facilities for legislators and staff are essential. Lawmakers should have places available where they might go for uninterrupted study, handling of mail, private discussions, and consultations. Staff effectiveness should not be limited by inadequate space, lack of resources, or the absence of mechanical assistance.

Legislative salaries must be considered if we are to obtain, encourage, and keep legislators who have a high degree of interest in public problems, maintain the respect of their communities, and can afford to spend considerable time with public responsibilities. The salary should be a respectable one, appropriate to attract knowledgeable, concerned individuals and compensate them at least somewhat for their time and loss of other income.

I am not suggesting here that we need full-time legislators. A part-time legislator maintains a degree of independence that I think is advantageous when he is not faced with having to win the next election to put bread and butter on his family's table. Being engaged in a vocation aside from his political endeavors increases his ability to "feel the pulse" of his district. One of the greatest shortcomings I see in congressmen today is that they have become full-time not only to their duties but full-time to Washington itself. It is too easy under those circumstances to become oblivious to local problems, needs, and views. I am satisfied that the so-called part-time legislator with adequate staffing can actually perform a better job than perhaps most of us could perform on a full-time basis.

In our attempts to develop and improve the legislative process, we often run into constitutional roadblocks and may be prone to blame our lack of progress on these constitutional provisions. Although constitutional change in many states may be a necessary and inherent part of legislative reform, we dare not use it as an excuse for delay. Not only can we recognize the constitutional problems and endeavor to seek amendments that will enhance opportunities for legislative reform, but in some instances we can also develop means to accommodate to uncomfortable constitutional provisions.

Obviously, the current role of state legislatures and the future development of their strength nationwide depends to a great extent upon their leadership and the function and role that leadership sees for its legislative body. Leadership should be strong enough not only to guide the legislative body itself, but to forcefully represent its viewpoint to the administrative branch of government and to represent effectively the legislative branch of government to the news media and the public as well.

It is paramount that legislative leaders recognize the need to restructure legislative procedures. There is hardly a place—in business or in community life—where people get more bogged down in tradition than in legislative bodies. The recognition of tradition should not overshadow the greater good of reorganization—a reorganization that need not detract from the *esprit* of the legislature, but in fact should enhance it. Nor should legislative leaders be satisfied that, by virtue of their leadership role, they are deeply involved in policy-making decisions of state government. Rank-and-file members of the legislature ought also to be involved in these decision-making processes.

If the potential for an expanded role in public policy determination for state government is to come about, it will be accomplished largely because of the desires expressed by and pressures brought from state capitals across this land—coupled with the demonstrated ability and capability to do the job. State legislatures ought to become more deeply involved on a national scale in working out, delineating, and establishing these new roles and responsibilities for state government *vis-à-vis* the federal government. We should encourage, perhaps insist, that legislative leaders devote a substantial portion of their time and effort in this regard. There has been only a minimum of coordinated effort along these lines. This is because it is difficult to motivate some legislative leaders: Some have reached their positions under an established system and do not want to risk rocking the boat in any regard; some are very satisfied to be a "big frog in their own little puddle"; and some are too preoccupied with a specific undertaking to become involved in the broader aspects of states' responsibilities. And too often, these leaders will hesitate to delegate and assign other members of their legislatures to undertake the role in their behalf.

If we suggest an expanded role and deeper involvement by the legislative branch, does this imply that we mean to encroach on the current role of some other branch of government, specifically the executive? I am sure most governors probably feel so. The attitude of legislators probably ranges from those who express almost a covetous view of the governor's role to those who may find themselves in particular favor with the chief executive, thereby fully satisfied with the relationship and in no mood to assert a prerogative of the legislature as a whole. I would think, however, that a legislature can be a more effective body and play a broader role without seeking to weaken the role of the executive, overtly at least.

There is no reason to spend time being jealous of the governor's role and the way in which he can exercise his functions. What legislators must do is candidly acknowledge practical, procedural, and legal factors, distinguishing the legislative and administrative branches. The governor is the single elected state-wide leader. He is the one who commands the attention of most of the news media and the public. He was elected to lead, and when he embarks upon a program it may be only after detailed study and development by the staff of his own office and the various departments involved, all out of public view, and then announced with a great deal of public attention and fanfare.

On the other hand, when a legislative matter is undertaken, a bill or perhaps several bills dealing with the same subject are introduced. They are referred to committees and perhaps sub-committees; differences are explored, alternatives weighed, usually all under the eye of the news media. This is a process that takes place in two separate houses of the legislature in all but one of our states.

For too long, legislative bodies, including to some extent the U. S. Congress, have been reactors not only to problems but to solutions and programs proposed by the executive branch. I would not deny that this is a role with which many legislators and legislative leaders throughout the country may be quite satisfied. But undoubtedly many of our state legislatures have accepted this secondary role simply because they are not equipped to formulate their own programs and proposals. Particular problems with which the legislature or some legislators are concerned should not have to await executive interest and attention.

Legislators have too great a tendency to decry the fact that they cannot command the type of public attention that the executive branch commands. But let's not fight it; let's recognize the diffcrences and recognize that we do not always have to compete. Handled properly, there is undoubtedly much more public attention members could draw to the legislative process, if they desired to do so. But we had better keep in mind that, as we invite attention, the news media might not be as selective as we would have them be in what they cover and report and in what their newspapers back home choose to print. We may often have to stand the scrutiny of a perhaps less-than-sympathetic press. The challenge is to make the press more understanding and not give it ready fodder to serve up to a potentially cynical public.

Do we not discern an increasingly cynical attitude toward government? Some politicians suspect that the point has been reached where many people almost expect those in government to be less than ethical, taking advantage of their political position for personal gain. If these attitudes are to be changed, legislators must not only avoid ethically questionable actions and substantive conflicts of interest—they must also avoid the appearances of these as well. I suppose every legislator, especially those who are part-time, has inherent conflicts of interest. The crucial matter is the nature and extent of them, the extent to which they influence views and actions, and how the legislature itself deals with them.

Some legislators find that their public position provides opportunities—including legal ones—for financial gain. They would rationalize that, after all, being in the legislature should not disqualify one from taking advantage of these opportunities. But as a matter of fact, if the opportunity—no matter how legitimate—comes about because of the legislator's position, then he may in fact be disqualified from these opportunities for financial gain as an ethical matter, at least in the eyes of the public. This may be considered an extreme view. But it is one that must be taken into consideration by any official who cares about public confidence. These conflicts may not be overlooked by the public. They should not be ignored by the legislature itself. A procedure for defining and dealing with substantive conflicts of interest and unethical actions should be a part of the structure of each legislative body.

The very attempts at reorganizing a legislative body depend to a great extent on how these attempts are viewed by the news media, and therefore the public. It is clear that legislators alone cannot accomplish reorganization; we need public support for some of the changes that we might want to undertake. We must, therefore, obtain the understanding and support of the media. One of the most effective ways is to encourage direct involvement of media personnel and public representatives in the review of legislative structure and organization and in the recommendation of changes. This has been done in several states through citizens' committees.

In summary, each state legislature should be an effective organization comprised of individuals who sincerely seek out the best course of action for their constituency and state. A legislature that recognizes its responsibilities and seeks to improve its methods of carrying them out is necessarily concerned about its image and public confidence. It has a leadership dedicated to an active legislative role in government, offers adequate salaries, staff, and facilities, and is ever willing to give attention to its shortcomings.

If state governments, and therefore state legislatures, are to have the opportunity of exercising greater influence in the affairs of government, I am convinced that they must first demonstrate their own capability to fulfill that role. This means that legislatures must be ever alert to the need for reform that strengthens their abilities to cope with contemporary situations demanding positive action.

These challenges are before us now; they are in fact opportunities that may never again come our way. If we achieve the position of assuming greater responsibilities—many of which have been or will be borne by the national government—I am confident that the net result will not necessarily be more government, but most assuredly better government.

From the Leader's Position . . .

JESS UNRUH

The famous Speaker of the House, Thomas Brackett Reed, was once asked by an indignant Democrat what he thought the rights of the minority party were. His answer was a trenchant summary of his own view of legislative leadership: "The right of the minority is to draw its salaries, and its function is to make a quorum." In those benighted days of powerful Speakers, it was not only possible, but realistic for Reed to make a comment like that and to add the somewhat more philosophical observation that "the best system is to have one party govern and the other party watch."

If Speaker Reed is now remembered as something more than a legislative "boss" it is because of his profound personal integrity. Of course, the fact that he was a Republican helped. As Harry Truman once said: "When a leader is in the Democratic party he's a boss; when he's in the Republican party he's a leader." Now it is doubtful that even Speaker Reed's rock-ribbed Republicanism would save him from the bossism charge if he were to attempt his tactics in Congress or in many state legislatures. His kind of frank partisanship, whether we like it or not, is out of fashion.

Today any effort to upgrade state legislatures depends on bipartisanship. The point needs emphasis. The success of any legislative modernization effort rests upon the groundwork that is laid. Anything that fragments and factionalizes is destructive. If, for example, the thrust for reform comes principally from only one house, it is all but impossible to overcome the apathy or open hostility of the executive branch.

The bipartisan approach is even more necessary if there is the obstacle of constitutional revision to overcome. Too many people already regard the state legislature as a cockpit for trivial controversy, more to be suffered than encouraged. If legislators cannot present a united front in an appeal for public support for their own institution, then it would be much better to postpone or abandon a campaign for reform, or at least adopt a piecemeal approach.

Furthermore, the appeal for financial support for such a campaign must be made to those interests that are closest to the legislature. Generally, these interests take an extremely narrow view of legislative reform. As does the governor, members of the third house [lobbyists] tend to believe that an increase in legislative competence somehow diminishes their own effectiveness. It requires the complete dedication of leaders of both parties in both houses to overcome these feelings. It can be fatal to permit outside forces to whipsaw a legislature internally, while it is engaged in a campaign on its own behalf.

Still other sources of important support in the public appeal for legislative reform are the so-called "good government" groups, such as the League of Women Voters, National Municipal League, and so forth. Usually, these groups demand bipartisanship.

Having emphasized the need for bipartisanship, it now becomes necessary to say something about how to achieve it. This is not so easy. In many states, the Thomas Brackett Reed approach to legislating is not an historical curiosity. There often is little more for the minority party to do than sit and watch the other party govern. The resulting sense of frustration is more likely to produce a desire for revenge than for reform.

It is difficult to determine whether the arrogance with which majority party leadership handles the minority stems from short-sightedness or supreme overconfidence, but it is usually repaid in kind when the minority replaces the majority. Having myself played that game, and then having decided to attempt some degree of accommodation with the minority, I can testify that the latter course is not only far more productive but also much more comfortable.

The minority party in the legislature, with a governor of the majority party, is just about useless if it is denied all the tools of quality decision making. But even if the governor is of the same political faith as the minority, the quality of the legislative product is immeasurably improved if the minority has independent staffing. I am not quite ready to say that the gulf between the parties is not so great as the gulf between the executive branch and the legislative in every instance and on every issue, but something like that is very nearly true as a general rule.

Except along broad philosophical or ideological lines, the interests of governors are rarely similar to those of members of their own party in the legislature. It has often seemed to me that the governor's principal interest in the legislators of his party is to use them as hatchet men on legislators of the opposition party. I do not quarrel with such an ancient political practice, but it presents dangerous implications for the legislature as an institution.

Legislatures are already factional by design—so much so that they appear incompetent and uncertain at the best of times. When legislative leaders are constantly quarrelsome, it cannot help but add to this image of incompetence. Certainly, argumentation is unavoidable in the necessary confrontation of the issues; but it ought to be confined or closely related to issues and subject matter. A legislator should be aware of the risks involved in attacking another legislator on behalf of the governor. He must be certain of the accuracy of his statements and have a healthy skepticism of the motives of the governor.

Internal legislative bickering can be ameliorated by adequate staffing. If legislators are not equipped with staff to scrutinize material provided by the executive, it is extremely unlikely that they can determine what is fact and what is fancy if the material deals with anything but the simplest and most obvious kind of issue.

The importance of staff can be illustrated by an experience in a past session of the California Legislature. The governor accused a legislative leader of the opposite party of stalling his economy program. The leader, who had an excellent staff, had a quick research job done that revealed that only one of the governor's twenty-two cost-cutting proposals had been introduced in his house and that the rest were languishing in the other chamber. He dutifully (if somewhat gleefully) informed the press of the inanity of the governor's charge. The governor then prepared a countercharge and asked the leader of his own party in the same house to issue it. This leader refused on the grounds that his own independent staff research indicated that the governor was, indeed, wrong. Had the legislative leader been incapable of doing the necessary research and accepted the statements of his own governor, he undoubtedly would have been trapped by the opposition party, and a legislative wrangle would have ensued. In the short run, one legislator might have been exposed as a dupe; but we cannot discount the long-run damage that this kind of uninformed dispute does to the legislature as a whole.

The dialogue over issues is immeasurably improved by minority party staffing. Useless partisan argument, either with the majority or the executive or both, is lessened. With staff and facilities, the minority can move intelligently, dissect proposals of the majority, and offer constructive amendment rather than simple obstinate obstruction. The minority then has a continuing involvement in the legislative process because of its capacity to originate its own proposals.

Independent staffing also has its effect upon minority-majority cooperation. When each party can participate jointly in the origination and development of a program and feel it has a stake in it, not only is the program's legislative road smoothed, but gubernatorial hostility is neutralized.

Again I draw on personal experience. In California, as in most major industrial states, the problem of hard-core unemployment is one of the most persistent and potentially explosive. The federal government continues to treat this problem as it did during the Depression, despite the fact that today's unemployment is entirely different in character. This has resulted in a growing pool of the chronically unemployed, constantly fed by the migration of unskilled rural workers and school dropouts.

Understanding the necessity for a drastic departure in dealing with this problem, the majority leadership undertook an extensive staff study. As this study was progressing, we learned that the minority staff was also concerned and had started some work of their own on the same problem. Quite naturally, the two staff projects merged, and a fruitful liaison developed. At this point, the leadership of both parties faced a necessity for choice. Each could go its separate way and develop its own program. The minority program would face the opposition of the majority, and the majority program would face the hostility of the governor. This, of course, is not all bad. Criticism and compromise could have improved whichever program survived. But this is not the course we took. Instead, we concentrated our efforts on producing one bipartisan package of legislation. As soon as these bills were introduced, they received the full support of the governor. So solid was the support for the program that it was able to survive the opposition of the U. S. Department of Labor. To be sure, neither party can now claim full credit for what will be an effective employment program in

California, but the sacrifice of a little glory and a few headlines is a small price to pay for forward-looking legislation.

Additionally, good staffing would free the leadership of concern with policy details and routine data analysis. The leaders would have more time to do the work of leadership—formulating broad policy, dealing directly with colleagues, and handling parliamentary procedure. This, after all, is what legislative leaders are elected to do.

No one else will be concerned with the legislative function if the leaders are not. Beyond a doubt, that function is enhanced by adequate facilities and staff. Generally, these resources will only be available in an atmosphere of mutual concern, cooperation, and respect between majority and minority leadership.

Insofar as the relationship between the leadership and other legislators is concerned, a change must take place too. Old systems of patronage and punishment to impose discipline are largely irrelevant. We can expect, I think, a new discipline based upon knowledge and competence. Equipped with facilities and staff, majority and minority leaders would be excellent sources of information for the members of their houses. They would be able to formulate policy intelligently and independently. The knowledge they command and the capacity to act and react quickly and accurately would be the tools with which the leadership would maintain this new legislative discipline.

All of this, of course, assumes a context of continuing legislative improvement. No legislative institution can grow very much without a parallel growth in the other institutions. This upgrading of our state legislatures is long overdue and not at all difficult to justify. Thirty years ago, a California governor had a "hot line" telephone installed at the Assembly speaker's rostrum so that he could issue his orders to the legislature personally, without the inconvenience of leaving his office. This "technological breakthrough" in the governmental process lasted only a short time. The legislature finally rebelled, and the new Speaker ceremoniously yanked the telephone wires out. I will always envy that

Speaker. Rarely does anyone holding public office have the opportunity to perform an act that is both so meaningful and so dramatic. That defiant act illustrates a profound philosophical truth. The major difference between a dictatorship and a democracy is an independent legislative branch.

We must admit that today many state legislatures, especially in the South, are still dominated by their governors. In Louisiana, for example, the governor appoints the chairmen and members of both the Senate and the House appropriations committees. Gubernatorial dominance is not the only threat. A weak, unequipped state legislature is an invitation to the federal government to undertake greater and greater responsibility for matters of day-to-day governmental concern. I am not one of those who views the federal government as a vast, malevolent force bent on destroying the traditional American way of life, but it is a fact that federal power is growing. We must resist this tendency of power to concentrate in one unit of government. The genius of the American political system is its unique equilibrium of forces, out of which solutions to our problems arise. In order to maintain this balance, state government must improve its competitive position.

Many of us who complain now about federal dominance and insensitivity must admit to a history of neglect of many of the problems that the federal government is trying to solve. This failure at the state level is truly regrettable, but contrition is of little value in confronting the problems that face us today. I believe that in a state that has demonstrated a capacity to initiate and carry out effective programs, federal legislation should permit the state government to control and further specify the way in which federal monies should be used. In this way, federal funds can assist a state to speed the implementation of its own carefully developed programs that go beyond minimum federal standards.

It would be impossible to predict, however, that such enlightenment at the federal level will take place. As we approach the great domestic problem of our time—the crisis in our cities—it appears that all the old mistakes will be repeated. For example, the federal government deals in many programs directly with local units of government. In most cases, the states have nothing to say about these programs beyond a flat veto. This should concern us, because it represents yet one more dilution of the power of state government, but it should concern us too because it is just plain inefficient.

When we speak of urban needs, we are not speaking of the needs of any one, clearly identifiable level of government. We are speaking of overlapping local jurisdictions, transportation problems, the organization of delivery systems for various services. Clearly we must go beyond the local level to solve problems, but this need not mean total dependence upon Washington. On the whole, the state has a much better picture of urban problems and their cross-jurisdictional implications than the federal government does. The state is also in a much better position to operate programs effectively. It can take a more flexible approach and design priorities on the basis of local conditions.

If we are to move beyond these theoretical assumptions, the states must demonstrate the capacity to solve urban problems. Some states—many states—should venture, experiment, and set the pace for the rest of the country. The states should exert a counterforce on the federal government to get its messy, uncoordinated house in order.

The pressure from the cities adds new urgency to the effort to revitalize our legislatures. Any large state with sizable urban problems requires regular annual sessions and the machinery for the legislature to call itself into session in response to crisis. Legislators must be willing to spend the time studying complex issues and must be equipped with the research and staff services needed. If legislators are to get closer to the problems of their constituents, they should be equipped with offices, not only in the state capitol, but in their home districts.

I have concentrated in this paper on the philosophical aspects of legislative leadership and largely ignored the more detailed, continuing demands of the job. This is a deliberate emphasis. Unless legislative leaders understand the philosophical underpinnings, they are unlikely to comprehend how to combat the massive inertia and apathy that confront them in the drive for legislative betterment.

It is difficult, of course, to assess the great differences between states and to synthesize accurately a leadership role that would be very meaningful for the disparate conditions that confront the fifty state legislatures. But there are several responsibilities of leadership that will add materially to the efficacy of the legislative performance.

First, there is the involvement of those individual members, whom Professor James D. Barber calls "lawmakers" and who, if not frustrated and driven out of the legislature by rigid and unconcerned leadership, can add materially to the process. Leadership should constantly be on the watch for the relatively few gifted people that the elective process supplies to the legislature and should attempt to reward them even if their views vary considerably from those of the leaders. This may necessitate elimination or modification of the seniority system or tradition, but the rewards of having intelligent, concerned, and committed secondary leadership are great. Not the least of these is better treatment by the communications media and consequent easing of the obstacles to legislative reform.

Second, there is a need for legislative leadership to adhere rigidly to the rules of the house, both written and understood. The temptation for the majority to deviate from those rules, because they are generally formulated to fortify the majority, can be lessened by consultation with minority leadership during the formative period. The penalty for not doing this can be session-long wrangling, and consequent harm to the legislative image. Conversely, if the minority leadership is given reasonable participation, one should reasonably be able to expect it to refrain from the temptation to use those rules as an excuse for irresponsibility. I cannot emphasize too much the need for the majority leadership to avoid shortcuts and to subscribe rigidly to the rules as agreed to. Variations, which are necessary once in a while, should only be resorted to after agreement with the minority leadership.

It goes almost without saying that leadership has the responsibility for seeing that the work flow is relatively constant and divided as evenly as it can be, that the calendar is kept moving, and that trivia on the floor is reduced to a minimum. Floor debate should be confined as much as possible to major substantive bills. Committee decisions should nearly always be made in full view of the public. Decorum on the floor will be encouraged if the time spent on minor matters is reduced to a minimum. A consent calendar to eliminate unnecessary motions on the floor has been helpful to some legislatures. Better attention to the details of smoothing out the floor operation will improve the over-all impression that the legislature creates and make major changes more acceptable.

We know that state legislatures have not in the past served as effectively as they should as forums for airing the problems of blacks and other minorities. The role our large cities once served in sociopolitical assimilation is being met less and less effectively, largely because of the altered composition of the population within the boundaries of the old cities. Thus, it seems to me, state legislatures should be developed and recognized as a meeting place, as a place of negotiation, and as a place for developing understanding among suburbanites and city-dwellers, among socio-economic classes, and among racial and ethnic groups.

There is a demonstrable loss of public confidence in our established political institutions. Many have remarked in recent years that we are behaving more and more like a Latin American republic. The public is unlikely to have confidence in our political system if it is remote and centralized in Washington, with bureaucratic blocks between public and programs and between public and policy makers. State legislatures, through the manifestation of knowledgeable concern with modern problems, can do much to relieve the anxiety and sense of frustration experienced by more and more of our citizens. This was the intent of the framers of our system of representative democracy. It is our responsibility and opportunity today.

From the Leader's Position . . .

ROBERT P. KNOWLES

Two or three years ago—even a year ago—the prescription for a typical enlightened discussion of state government and the state legislature went something like this: Legislatures must assert themselves. They must sharpen their tools, revamp their procedures, streamline their techniques, improve their decision-making abilities, and thrust themselves into what we have been constantly describing as a coordinate role in government.

I suspect that hundreds, perhaps thousands, of speeches, papers, and articles have been prepared around these basic points. Every one of us who has the remotest kind of exposure to the legislature has heard or read them. For even more years, we have been literally bombarded with the statistics of our failures and catalogues of our shortcomings. To be sure, most of these descriptions have been accompanied by suggested remedies. The remedy for archaic procedures, for instance, is to update the procedures. The remedy for disgraceful compensation is to increase the compensation. The remedy for unresearched decision is researched judgment.

The files of every legislative reference library, legislative council, university political science department, and government organization are stuffed with the prescriptions designed to right what has obviously been wrong. And these are not to be deprecated or belittled. Most of them are valid, most of them are logical, and most of them are useful. They are well-written, well-documented, and well-directed.

But in all truth, little has been accomplished. We have seen in recent years an astounding growth of interest from the academic community. We can today find support in university after university for the proposition that state legislatures are in need of reform and remodeling. We have begun to take our case to business and industry, and we have found a sympathetic ear time after time. We have told the private sector of our communities that they must become interested in this movement, and they have agreed and responded. And still we have not gotten very far.

The great crusade toward modernizing the state legislature has at this point been something less than a howling success. Where giant strides are needed, only a few legislatures have taken halting steps. The need for reform is generally recognized today by the press, by citizen groups, by the business and academic community, and by legislators themselves. Progress is being made at a snail's pace, if at all. And in today's world we cannot travel at that pace, for the problems multiply faster than the solutions.

We have been inundated with *what* is wrong, and *what* should be done. But nobody has as yet come up with the *how*. And that is the key to the riddle. Large sectors of the American public agree on what is wrong, and there is a vast weight of influential opinion as to what needs to be done. But nobody is talking about *how* to do it.

This assessment may sound pessimistic; yet we do have the tools and the ability to do what must be done. Despite a lack of visible progress, we have come a long way. When men like Jess Unruh started talking about this problem a few years ago, nobody was even listening, let alone reacting. All that has changed. We have rounded a corner, although we might not realize it. If we have indeed successfully imparted the idea of a need for reform, and an outline of the boundaries of that reform, then it is essential that we go ahead. The American political scene is not a portrait; it is a moving parade, and the participants who are coming down the block today will be moving away tomorrow, to be replaced by others.

The professors and the businessmen and the editors can illuminate our way and pile up our statistics. But nobody can reform the legislature except legislators. Until the day the legislators in any given state decide that they will improve their own institutions, the best-intentioned editorials, citizen studies, and academic documentations will gather dust on the shelves of the library. On the other hand, when the legislators do decide to act, nothing can block that action for long.

This is a task—perhaps the greatest task—for legislative leadership; and the National Conference of State Legislative Leaders has firmly recognized it. But it need not be exclusively the prerogative of the leadership, for many times it is the leadership itself that most strenuously resists reform. When the tide is right, vigorous young legislators with vision can recognize it just as well as can seasoned veterans.

The tools are all around us. There are in print a number of outstanding proposals and studies directed toward the problems of the legislature. As far back as 1954, the American Political Science Association published Professor Belle Zeller's definitive study *American State Legislatures*. Most of the recommendations are as valid today as they were then. In 1961, the National Legislative Conference, a group supported by the Council of State Governments, issued the final report and recommendations of its committee on Legislative Processes and Procedures, titled *American State Legislatures in Mid-Twentieth Century*. Every state has copies of that report; in some few states a portion of the recommendations have been implemented. But once again, on balance it remains a blueprint for modernization that has not yet been enacted. In that same year a printed discussion-outline called "Improving Legislative Procedures," compiled to give direction to the annual meeting of the National Conference of State Legislative Leaders, publicized many areas of legislative improvement. In 1963 the Committee on Organization of Legislative Services of the National Legislative Conference distributed its final report, "Mr. President . . . Mr. Speaker." This, too, is available to all the states, and in 1966 the Conference by formal resolution admonished the states to utilize the information contained in its report and in other publications. The following year the Committee for Economic Development reported on legislative improvement. Because of the prestige of the committee, this report has received more widespread publicity than any of the others. Yet the recommendations are anything but new.

These publications were all widely distributed, and most of them are still available. Furthermore, at least thirty states in recent years have undertaken studies of one kind or another concerned with staffing, procedures, and organization, and have made specific recommendations. Thus no one can say that the movement for modernization of the legislature suffers from lack of information. As mentioned earlier, the *what*, the *what's wrong*, and the *what ought to be done* have been adequately covered, to say the least.

Briefly, the goals set forth in all these studies and publications can be summarized as follows:

1. Legislative-executive relations need improvement in such areas as the presession evolution of public policy and the preparation of the legislative program, appropriation of public funds and the postaudit of public expenditures, and review of administrative rules and decisions, retaining in the legislature some control over the powers that it delegates to administrative agencies.

2. Legislative sessions should be free of undue restriction with regard to length of session, frequency of meetings, and subject matter to be discussed. The proposition that all of a state's

problems can be solved in a three-month session held once every two years is not plausible any more. Moreover, there are indications that holding one general session and one budget session in each biennium has not come up to the expectations of its proponents. It is no solution.

3. Legislative compensation should be specified by statute rather than by constitution. Legislative salaries should be based on the responsibilities of the job of a legislator as compared to that of a head of a division in the executive branch. They should be high enough to attract to legislative service qualified persons from all walks of life. In a recent study, the Committee for Economic Development states that even in the smaller states the legislator's salary should be fifteen thousand dollars, while in larger states it might be set as high as twenty-five thousand dollars.

4. Legislative staff should be selected on the basis of merit and competence. The type of information needed by a state legislature may differ from that needed by other branches of state government; but the information needs of the policy-setting branch of state government are at least as critical as those of the administrative branch. The legislature should provide itself with sufficient (and full-time) staff so that it can meet its information needs on a continuing basis.

5. Legislative standing committees should be assigned broad functional areas of subject-matter responsibility. This will make it possible for their members to specialize and to develop expertise in the area of committee responsibility. To some degree (if the number of standing committees is held small enough) it will eliminate time conflicts in the committee schedule. The citizen interested in legislation will be better able to attend the hearings of importance to him. All major proposals should receive public hearings, and notices of public hearings should be published early enough to enable interested parties to attend.

6. All legislative measures and amendments thereto should be printed. They should be available for distribution before public

hearings are held. All legislative measures prior to printing should be inspected by a professional bill-drafting staff. Where one legislature holds several successive sessions throughout its term of office, provision should be made for the carry-over of proposals from one session to the next throughout the term. This saves staff time, printing time, and printing costs. Every legislature should make adequate provision for the printing and distribution of new laws before they become effective.

7. State legislatures, and their staffs, should explore all modern business machines and techniques for possible application to the legislative process. There are possibilities of improving the flow of legislative work by using machines for roll-call voting, re-production of legislative measures, preparation of journals, in-dexing, bill status, information retrieval, statute law research, recording of public hearings, and legislative debates. With the text of the statutes stored in memory, computers can speed up bill typing, engrossing, enrolling, the publication of slip laws, and the editing and publication of the revised statutes.

8. Legislative finances—the funding of the operation of the legislature itself—are in need of review. State legislatures should provide themselves with appropriations adequate to meet all probable expenditures during a fiscal period. They should have exclusive control over these finances, and should exercise that control responsibly.

9. Office facilities outside the chambers of the legislature, and sufficient staff individually assigned, should be available to every legislator. The measure of what is "sufficient" may differ from state to state. But members of state legislatures should not have to put up with working conditions which, individually, they would not tolerate in their private business or profession.

10. Orientation aids and presession seminars should offer to all members of state legislatures the opportunity to familiarize themselves—before the beginning of a new legislative term—with the services available to them and the rules under which they will have to work.

This summary could, of course, be extended and probably is being extended in some of the states today. But it pretty well covers the basic points we have all been making, and reading about, for the past several years.

With all this to build upon, why haven't we progressed further? The answer, as noted earlier, lies in the fact that we have not come to grips with the *how* of legislative modernization. We are up to our eyeballs in the "what"; we are awash in the "things to do" field. But we don't know how to do it.

There are three rather basic steps that we must take to achieve the *how*. First, we must build or engender the inspiration and desire to do something. Second, we must know what needs to be done in each individual state and how to do it. And third, we must develop public support.

The first step—the development of inspiration and desire— is the hardest. There is, despite all we have seen and heard, still great resistance to change within the legislature itself. Many of our legislators, particularly the ones who have been around the longest and have the stature and know-how to lead the drive, are perfectly satisfied with things the way they are. In many states it is the legislative leadership itself that blocks reform. For instance, a Speaker may very well be opposed to a proposal to reduce the number of committees, since this would reduce the number of appointments he can make, and thus reduce the number of legislators obligated to him.

Yet the inspiration for modernization must come from within the legislature itself. It cannot be imposed from the outside. It is unlikely that any of us will see the day when an aroused citizenry will demand higher pay for the legislature, nor for that matter, enlarged staff or better facilities. There may be a few sympathetic editorials written, a Chamber of Commerce resolution passed, and the support pledged of the League of Women Voters. But it won't *really happen* unless it happens within the legislative halls themselves.

The desire and the imagination need not await the inclinations of the leadership in every case. Although it may appear heretical for a leader to advocate movement from below, reform can often-times be brought about more quickly and more enthusiastically when it is the result of the fresh, unjaundiced, often idealistic inspiration of a new legislator. Harold Katz, for instance, took a look at the Illinois legislature in his first term and said: "We simply can't operate the state of Illinois in this fashion." He didn't exactly win any popularity contests with his leadership or his colleagues in the beginning, but the Katz Commission made rapid strides toward modernization in that body.

The second key factor in developing our *how to* is knowledge, and I have previously indicated that we are overwhelmed by knowledge. But the fact that all this has accumulated and little has happened leads to the conclusion that something is missing. One of the missing items is competition, which does not exist and probably never will exist among states and state legislatures. The reason a private business constantly sharpens its tools and hones its procedures is that if it does not the fellow down the street will put it out of work.

The publications and the studies and the papers of individual state legislatures, by and large, fall short of describing a model legislature, and they are not inclined to be inspirational. Ideally, Wisconsin should send a team of knowledgeable legislators and adequate staff to every state in the Union, to study every legisla-ture and bring the best ideas home for application to Wisconsin. But this is impractical.

The next best thing, in my opinion, is the development of the Center for State Legislative Research and Service, which the NCSLL and the Eagleton Institute of Politics put together at Rutgers. The day should come when this center will be not only a first-rate library of information for the legislators of any state, but the repository of Eagleton studies performed in every state of the nation by real experts. Then we will have it all in one place, and Wisconsin can be measured against West Virginia, to see whether and where Wisconsin could do better and could innovate. In this manner, we would approach a working description of the model state legislature.

Third, having created the desire and followed it with the Eagleton-type study, we must have the public support to put it through. Here is a place for the skill of the Citizens Conference on State Legislatures, with its close contacts in the business and academic communities. Here is the place where the growing science of public relations must be brought to bear.

Recently in Wisconsin, the need for a pay increase became evident to the legislators. The desire was there. Information was available to show it was possible and practical. But at that point we passed the ball to a citizens' group, a respected committee of business leaders. They spent a good deal of time interviewing every legislator and most other elected and appointed officials who had ever served in or with the legislature. They concluded that a legislator's job in Wisconsin at full-time effort should be worth fifteen thousand dollars annually. They concluded that the Wisconsin legislator, other than leaders, was spending 53 percent of his time at his legislative job. Therefore they applied the 53 percent to the $15,000 and announced the resulting figure to the press. The higher salary sailed through with hardly a ripple of dissent.

This year Wisconsin became the first state in the nation to modernize, streamline, and completely reorganize the structure of the administrative branch of government. The reorganization was accomplished by the legislature, without executive order or any action by the governor. It was done by bill and statute, reducing some eighty-seven agencies into thirteen departments and a few related boards. It was done because prominent citizens sat on the committee with legislators, and then fought for the committee bill, in public and in the press.

California legislators in 1966 achieved a pay increase to sixteen thousand dollars, by coupling a conflict-of-interest amendment with the pay raise in a referendum. North Carolina built a seven-million-dollar legislative building, and the whole state is proud of it. And this is how it goes when *public support* is there.

More than any other institution except perhaps the schools, the legislature is a creature of the people, and it is rightfully sensitive to public opinion. When we move toward legislative reform, we must learn not to cringe from the public, but to enlist its support—and this can always be done if our proposals are sound.

Thus it seems that the way to translate into reality all the proposals for more effective legislatures is to instill inspiration and desire, provide the knowledge, and enlist the support of the public. If we can do these three things, then we can begin to turn all the articles, books, and studies into solid achievement.

part three
STRATEGIES AND
TACTICS OF REFORM

Strategies and Tactics of Reform
An Introduction

ALAN ROSENTHAL

Granted the urgency of legislative reform, why and how does it actually come about? Any number of factors help explain the impetus for and the success of improvement campaigns. Of importance today are general pressures from outside the state. Discussions of legislative reform at conferences of leaders and rank-and-file and the examples set by one legislature after another shape the contemporary environment in which legislatures exist. Sometimes there are intense citizen demands from within a state, which persuade legislative leadership to undertake reform activity on its own. Frequently critical events are largely responsible for reform. Reapportionment, which brings in a large number of new and younger members, has been extremely significant in many states. Occasionally a shift in party control in the state or of the governorship prompts a drive for a stronger legislative branch. In some places a political leader emerges, and he makes reform a central concern. Some legislatures undertake improvement out of a sense of extreme deprivation; others undertake it because of deep-rooted traditions of governmental reform.

Usually a number of factors come into play, and it is hazardous to offer generalizations that apply to every case and cover every state. In Part Three of this volume several contributors do generalize, recognizing nonetheless differences and exceptions from place to place. The task they set themselves is the exploration of strategies and tactics in the contemporary movement toward legislative reform.

I

Strategies and tactics are shaped largely by the obstacles to reform that must be overcome and the limited resources available with which to overcome them. When one takes into account the obstacles that exist, it seems remarkable that so much, rather than so little, has been accomplished during the past decade.

Whether we like it or not, "the dominant truth to be known about legislative reform . . . [is] that only a few people at any one time really care about it. . . ." These are the words of William J. Keefe, a professor of political science and chairman of his department at the University of Pittsburgh. In his essay, Professor Keefe portrays the backdrop of massive indictment of the legislative institution. Given such a setting, it would be surprising if the general public, no matter how urgent the need, would become very aware of or concerned about legislative improvement. Charles O. Davis, who has been closely involved with reform as executive secretary of the National Conference of State Legislative Leaders and whose essay also appears in Part Three, agrees that public indifference must be overcome.

The problem is not only public indifference. There is also gubernatorial indifference, or even hostility. Earlier we suggested that state legislatures should accept the responsibility for strengthening executive institutions, since this is in their interests as well as the state's. Governors can be relied on to do the opposite. Only a few have devoted energy or initiative to the tasks of strengthening legislatures. Unfortunately, as Professor Keefe remarks, "the typical governor is likely to believe that a weak legislature is likely to serve his interests better." In my own opinion, reflected in the essay that appears below, governors are natural opponents of legislative modernization. There are several reasons for this: Some governors believe in the executive-force model of government, and simply do not conceive of a co-equal role for the legislature; others feel that their own authority may be diminished as a consequence of legislative strengthening; many are satisfied with the status quo, and are not willing to risk new arrangements; and a few find it convenient to use their legislatures as scapegoats, in order to derive personal, political advantage.

Gubernatorial opposition, however, need not discourage a purposeful legislature. There are ways of recruiting support from attentive citizens and neutralizing the governor. There are ways also of meeting his overt opposition head on. In both Florida and Connecticut, for example, legislatures took on their governors, enacted improvement bills, overrode vetoes, and survived the heat that ensued. A governor's hostility, in fact, may indirectly promote the cause of legislative reform. His attacks can engender a sense of institutional identity that a legislature might otherwise be unable to achieve. Ironically, perhaps, a battle with a governor may have a more enduring effect than the legislative reforms that may have prompted the battle.

It would be encouraging if the press would rally to the cause of legislative reform. But today the press in most states is a weak reed on which to rely. For the most part, state legislatures are poorly covered by the capital press corps. In addition, as Charles O. Davis charges, "most newspapers have an abysmal understanding of what a legislature really is." The press probably does not understand because the legislature's untidiness is troublesome; by contrast, the hierarchical executive is orderly, comprehensible, and easier to report on in a brief, hurried news story. In addition, as Professor Keefe charges, "there are some grounds for believing that the press would rather have an exciting issue to report than major, though quiet, accomplishment."

An appropriate strategy involves the education of the press. During the past few years this effort has been undertaken by the Citizens Conference on State Legislatures. Recognizing the need for an informed and concerned public and the critical mediating role of the press, CCSL launched a program of news media conferences, designed to increase media awareness of the need for legislative improvement and to solicit cooperation in relating the story to the public. Since 1967, nine conferences, bringing together representatives of the news media as well as civic and legislative leaders, have been held, with participation by twenty-one states.

But the blame, of course, is not completely with the press. It is shared by the legislature itself. Although many individual members have excellent relationships with capitol reporters and receive the kind of coverage they deserve, the legislature has greater difficulty, particularly on matters of institutional change. Too frequently, this is due in large part to legislative secretiveness, which stems from the belief that when information becomes public it hurts rather than helps. I doubt that, if a legislature is serious about improvement, this will really be the case. Thus an obvious strategy emerges: In order to obtain adequate and fair coverage of reform campaigns, legislatures will have to take greater pains to inform reporters—and inform them earlier—about just what is being considered and why.

II

If there is a single principal obstacle to reform, however, it is the legislature. A telling remark, repeated at conferences of legislative leaders and members, echoes the comic-strip character

Pogo: "We have met the enemy and he is us." Because of factors over which it has only some control, the legislature may be the enemy of itself. Improvement comes hard for a number of reasons.

First, in most states institutional awareness and loyalty are minimal. Service is part-time and often temporary, while professions and occupations tend to be full-time and permanent. In some states, where legislative bodies meet infrequently or members commute to the capitals from their homes, institutional identification is entirely lacking. Second, members even at work have many issues other than reform with which to occupy themselves. They must legislate, deal with representatives of the executive branch and interest groups, and run errands for constituents. Moreover, as Charles O. Davis remarks, "the most intense pressure for reform of the legislature almost always arises precisely at the time when the legislature is most occupied with agonizing problems." Reform is put at the bottom of the agenda, while immediate, pressing issues are placed at the top. Third, legislators, like other human beings, are reluctant to abandon the familiar and risk the uncertain. They too are creatures of habit, not anxious to change a system they think they have mastered. Fourth, many changes lead to a redistribution of power. Professor Keefe observes: "Some legislative leaders and some rank-and-file members are likely to be chary of change because they think that they will be worse off in power terms if change is made." Few politicians want to see their own power diminished.

It would be foolish to suppose that there are simple ways of overcoming these obstacles. But certain strategies seem generally appropriate. All are based, in one fashion or another, on the recognition that reform is a fragile commodity, and to achieve change, and especially to make it work, there has to be a high degree of consensus within the legislature itself. This means that differences between senior and junior members, those from urban and rural districts, liberals and conservatives, representatives and senators, and Democrats and Republicans will have to be surmounted. Sometimes this cannot be done, but sometimes also the prophecy that it is fruitless even to try becomes self-fulfilling.

Take partisanship, for instance. Contributors to this volume are in fundamental agreement. Jess Unruh and Robert P. Knowles mentioned earlier the need for bipartisanship in reform campaigns. William J. Keefe comments that if reform proposals are dramatized as the inspiration of simply one party, they run a good risk of becoming tainted. Charles O. Davis emphasizes that no legislature can become more effective unless the effort is essentially bipartisan. Observe the contrast, mentioned in my essay, between the successful cooperation of two parties in Connecticut on the one hand and the failure of a partisan minority and a rigid Speaker to compromise in Wisconsin on the other.

Few people, whether public servants or not, can be expected to disregard their own personal well-being and interests. Legislators are no exception. This means that insofar as possible, the advantages and disadvantages of improvement should be rather equally distributed within the legislature. Only the legislature itself should come out significantly ahead.

Consider a concrete problem: a reduction in the number of standing committees. If there are fewer committees, there will be fewer chairmanships, and chairmanships even of inactive committees do confer status. There are ways of coping with the situation. If turnover of incumbent chairmen is high—because some retire, others are dissuaded from running by formidable challengers, and still others are defeated in primary or general elections—the opportunity to consolidate committees is obvious. But if tenure is stable and nevertheless fewer committees are desirable, the bull may have to be taken by the horns. Deprived of their status when their committees are eliminated, former chairmen can be allowed to retain some perquisites. Indemnity is possible. Not only is there the gratitude of legislative colleagues, but there is the secretary, the desk or office, the subcommittee chairmanship, the assignment to a major committee, and other perquisites legislative leaders can offer to compensate for loss.

Whatever the internal roadblocks, institutional reform is primarily the responsibility of legislators themselves. At some point, either earlier or later, they will have to become involved and decide on the future. This is exactly as it should be, for legislators, better than anyone else, according to Professor Keefe, "know what it is all about, know what the stakes are, know where opportunities exist, know what is feasible and what is not, and know how legislative careers are going to be affected by legislative processes."

If legislators have the major responsibility, legislative leaders bear the main burden. "What they elect to do, or are pressured into doing," Professor Keefe continues, "will determine how the legislature looks, how it goes about its business, and how significant a role it plays in the political system." It is not much of an exaggeration to say, as does Charles O. Davis in his essay, that without the involvement or at least the acquiescence of the leadership, there will be no important change in the state legislature.

But what are the leader's stakes in reform? They are not to increase his position and power at the expense of other members. Rather they are to increase the legislature's collective power with respect to other state institutions and to improve its overall performance with regard to state programs and policies; for a leader's real power in state government, Mr. Davis writes, depends on his leading "a body of reasonable, knowledgeable, responsible legislators" and not being "the chieftain of an ignorant tribe whom nobody respects." Thus, in helping to provide his members with the capability of exercising power themselves, Mr. Davis continues, "the leader finds he has not given up power at all, but has built understanding and a stronger power base."

There is probably no better example of this than the ex-

perience of Jess Unruh in California. As Speaker he did much
to strengthen the California Assembly, improve its committees,
and increase the competence and hence the independence of
individual members. Yet his own prerogatives and power suffered
not at all; he managed to exercise leadership, maintain control,
and fashion a national reputation in the process. The timid
and the insecure may not believe it, but what leaders mainly
stand to lose as a consequence of legislative reform is their
own powerlessness.

III

For the timid or the strong, resources from outside are available. Although the contribution outsiders can make is limited,
their support of legislative insiders can be of substantial help
in achieving reform. Charles O. Davis, as have other contributors
to this volume, mentions organizational, academic, and citizen
resources available to legislatures that are ready to move. Mr.
Davis notes that the National Conference of State Legislative
Leaders—which was established in 1959, and since then has
held conventions, sponsored special meetings, and undertaken
other activities—is an important resource for leaders who need
to know more about reform. Two groups, which are referred
to frequently in these essays, merit a brief digression. Their
activities illustrate how those outside who work with those within
can help identify problems, generate solutions, mobilize the
legislature, and rally the attentive public.

Among varied activities, the Eagleton Institute, through its
center for state legislative research and service, has undertaken
on a contractual basis studies for seven legislatures since late 1966.
Comprehensive reports were submitted to Rhode Island and Maryland in 1967, to Wisconsin and Connecticut in 1968, to Florida
and Mississippi in 1969. A detailed study of interim work was sub-

mitted to the Texas Senate in 1971. In these endeavors, no attempt was made to transform the political systems of the states;
but instead these were taken as given, and concentration was on
changes that seemed both desirable and relatively feasible. The
goals were to encourage legislators to think seriously about their institution, offer a constructive program for improvement, and
have the program—or important parts of it—adopted.

Operating on the assumption that each state is different,
and consequently the problems and needs of one legislature
might be quite unlike those of another, Eagleton has used
several techniques in its explorations. First, its staff has worked
closely with legislative leaders or special legislative committees,
since it was deemed vital that legislators themselves participate
in deliberations on and formulation of proposals for reform.
Second, a member of the staff was located at the state capitol,
so that as thorough a familiarity as possible with the atmosphere
and less formal practices of the legislature could be obtained.
Third, members and staff of the legislature, reporters from the
press, officials of the executive branch, and representatives of
citizens groups all were interviewed. In the six states where comprehensive studies were conducted more than 450 legislators were
asked for their views, and many of them were interviewed more
than once. The studies that resulted explored virtually every aspect
of the legislative process. Proposals in each state were quite specific.
In Rhode Island, there were 59 recommendations; in Maryland,
92; in Wisconsin, 183; in Connecticut, 108; in Florida, 79; and in
Mississippi, 103.

Among varied activities, the Citizens Conference on State
Legislatures has encouraged and supported citizens commissions
in nineteen states since its program started in 1965. The goal
of CCSL in its work with state commissions is to emphasize
the need for legislative improvements. The 1969 annual report
of the Conference advances the rationale underlying its effort:

> Legislative leaders are often aware of the restrictions under which
> they try to operate. Political factors may make it difficult or im-

practical for them to act. The voting public, which has the ulti-
mate authority to remove state constitutional restrictions on the
legislature, deserves to be made aware of the consequences of
maintaining the status quo versus the creative potential of clearing
the legislative decks for action.

In order to get the job in the states done, CCSL has provided
background and research materials, aided in the tasks of citizen
education and media involvement, sought editorial support, so-
licited the advice and cooperation of interest groups, counseled
state commissions and occasionally provided some funds for
their operations, and generated momentum to ensure that recommended reforms were incorporated into new constitutional or
statutory provisions.

Most recently, both groups have undertaken a number of other
major innovative projects. The Citizens Conference in early 1971
completed a fourteen-month study evaluating and ranking the fifty
state legislatures according to their decision-making capacities. It
is now in the process of launching a model committee staffing
scheme, which will be applied in several state legislatures. At the
same time, Eagleton is beginning two three-year demonstration
projects—one in cooperation with the Connecticut General Assembly to develop an effective system of "legislative review and
evaluation," and the other in cooperation with a number of legislators from about six northeastern states to develop better methods
for the "formulation of state programs."

What difference has the work of Eagleton and CCSL made?
It is too early to adequately assess impact. Certainly, these
efforts have contributed to the dialogue and placed legislative
reform higher on the agenda of the states. Even more important, these campaigns for legislative improvement have helped
strengthen identification with the legislature, and this—perhaps as
much as anything else—can help strengthen the legislature.

If action can be taken as a standard, there have been some
promising results thus far. Most of Eagleton's recommendations
were adopted within two sessions by the Rhode Island General

Assembly. This did not solve the legislature's problems, but progress was made. In Maryland key recommendations were accepted: standing committees were consolidated in the House of Delegates, the fiscal staff and budget review were buttressed, and improved interim work by committees may be at hand. A beginning—albeit a modest one—has been made in Mississippi. By contrast, in Florida, improvement was well under way when the legislature commissioned Eagleton to conduct a study. Florida surely would have pushed forward in any case, but the Eagleton presence and report undoubtedly proved to be of some assistance. Meanwhile, citizens commissions in a number of states have had demonstrable success.

The experience of Connecticut is a case in point. It is an excellent example of legislative initiative and interorganizational cooperation. The Connecticut General Assembly had made little progress over the years. Traditionally, it depended on direction furnished by the governor, executive branch, and state party leaders. By 1967, due largely to reapportionment, the legislature was ready to break the bonds of habitual subservience. Together with a group of concerned citizens, the state League of Women Voters, the Citizens Conference, and the Eagleton Institute, the legislature set about the business of major improvement.

CCSL provided matching funds, and the legislature hired Eagleton to undertake a year-long study. A citizens commission was established and the state League of Women Voters sponsored a presession orientation conference for Connecticut legislators. In October and November 1968, the League made a series of recommendations; in December the Eagleton report was submitted; and the following May the state Citizens Conference offered its proposals to improve the General Assembly.

Most definitely, 1969 was a vintage year in Connecticut, as the legislature moved with purpose and speed. In January it adopted new rules, designed to streamline and enhance the effectiveness of legislative procedures. In May it approved a proposed constitutional amendment to add a three-month session during even years to the existing five-month session during odd years. In June it passed a bill creating a leadership committee on legislative management and providing for professional legislative staff agencies. This bill was vetoed by the governor the following month; but nine days later, in an amazing display of independence, the legislature overrode the veto by unanimous votes in both the Senate and the House. During 1970, the Citizens Conference on the General Assembly reactivated itself to spearhead the campaign for ratification of the annual-session amendment. The amendment was ratified in November. Meanwhile, the legislature began to hire professional staff, develop a student internship program, and strive for more effective activity by standing committees during interim periods.

IV

Connecticut was remarkable; in a different way so was Maryland. A most serious obstacle to legislative reform, as William J. Keefe and others point out, is the state constitution, which restricts just what the legislature can do for itself or for the people it represents. The failure of the constitution proposed by a Maryland convention in 1968 is an unhappy illustration of a few of the themes we have discussed above. Howard Penniman, a professor of government at Georgetown University, was a delegate to the convention and an ardent backer of the constitution that emerged. In his essay, Professor Penniman describes the workings of the convention and the inclusion of significant legislative reforms in the proposed draft. If adopted, the new constitution would have: reduced the size of both houses of the Maryland General Assembly; provided for moving toward single-member districts and away from multimember ones; extended the length of legislative sessions; raised salaries of members;

increased the powers of the legislature; and eliminated the need for the legislature to enact detailed local legislation.

Despite the over-all excellence of the proposed constitution, it was defeated overwhelmingly by the voters of Maryland. Professor Penniman analyzes the nature of citizen support and opposition, and explains that many citizens "voted only their fears, and the consequences were devastating for reform." Legislative improvements were defeated because they were linked in one package to other and more emotional items. Unless the issues are framed correctly, the electorate cannot really be counted on, especially in times when social tension is high and people feel inclined to express their frustrations by negative votes at the polls. Professor Penniman concludes from the Maryland experience that an appropriate strategy of change will eschew a constitutional convention that submits its entire work to the voters in one piece. A convention can work out proposals and draft legislative reforms, but then they should be submitted separately for ratification by the electorate. For him, the piecemeal approach, as followed in Pennsylvania and Virginia, is the most productive one to take. "It does not force the voters into an all-or-nothing choice," he writes, "and it does not allow the accumulation of grievances. . . ."

The lessons derived from the failure in Maryland—as well as those in Rhode Island and New York, where entire constitutions were rejected by the voters—have not gone unheeded. Most recently, the trend has been toward the establishment of constitutional commissions and the decision to attempt constitutional reform by piecemeal amendment instead of by wholesale revision. Traditionally, the great majority of states employed constitutional conventions for major overhaul. But the situation has changed radically. As reported by the Council of State Governments, during 1968–69, of 490 amendments proposed, only 7 percent were initiated by constitutional conventions, while 92 percent were initiated by legislative bodies (and another

1 percent resulted from popular initiative). Legislative articles continued to be improved. During this period, of all the amendments proposed, sixty-eight concerned the legislative branch. And of these, as many as fifty-two were ratified and incorporated into state constitutions.

Another case that illustrates a number of the themes previously discussed is provided by legislative reform in Illinois. We hope that the Illinois experience will be a more common one than the Maryland experience. Harold A. Katz, a member of the Illinois House of Representatives and chairman of the Commission on the Organization of the General Assembly, describes just what was done in his legislature. In 1965, with the House controlled by Democrats and the Senate controlled by Republicans, a bill with bipartisan support created a commission on the General Assembly. Membership on the commission was well balanced: three members from the majority and two from the minority party in each chamber; ten public members appointed by legislative leaders; and the Speaker and president pro tempore *ex officio*. The value of outside support was evidenced as the commission received assistance from the faculty of state universities and other experts who served as consultants. The state appropriated thirty thousand dollars for the commission's work, and contributions from the public added 13,300 dollars more.

Representative Katz details how the commission, after thorough hearings and deliberation, showed just what bipartisan cooperation could accomplish. It offered a total of eighty-seven recommendations for improvement, of which eighty-four were unanimously supported by commission members. (A number of these recommendations, Representative Katz points out, were the outgrowth of unhappy incidents that had occurred in the legislature.) The question was then whether the proposals would be adopted.

With a change in the legislative balance—the Democrats having lost their majority in the Illinois House—there was concern whether the new leadership would go along with the commission's report. The leadership did, and despite some objection within the legislature to "change for change's sake," seventy-two of the eighty-seven recommendations were adopted in whole or in part within four years of their presentation.

In Illinois, Representative Katz concludes, the commission composed of both legislators and public members worked well, partly because of the full participation of the legislative leadership. As we have mentioned, there are other formats, other strategies, and other tactics. What will work best depends largely on local conditions and specific circumstances.

V

The adoption of reforms in the Illinois legislature or elsewhere is only the beginning. Unfortunately, there is a tendency to concentrate on the formulation and adoption of improvement programs, and then leave implementation to a rather dreary fate. Making reforms work so that they accomplish something worthwhile is troublesome. But it is absolutely necessary for the legislature to shoulder the responsibility for effective implementation, even after it has carried the burden of adoption.

Nor should we delude ourselves into believing that organizational and operational changes, whether overwhelmingly adopted or skillfully implemented, will solve the legislature's problems. The legislature's problems will never be solved—not as long as legislatures survive—nor should they be. The need for change and improvement will continue. What was appropriate yesterday and what works today may well be ineffectual tomorrow. There is no end to institutional reform.

Reform and
the American Legislature

WILLIAM J. KEEFE

The American state legislature today is in trouble—this seems
to be the main theme in commentary about state government.
Critics of the legislature are numerous: the press, portions of
the academic world, a variety of interest groups that believe
they have been disadvantaged, the governor, mayors of assorted
cities, elements within state bureaucracies, the popular journals,
the courts, the indifferent public, and the attentive public. Not
all the critics are on the outside looking in. Occasionally in
some states, and frequently in others, state legislators themselves are hostile witnesses concerning the legislative institution.
It is very possibly true that no American political institution
has ever had so many detractors, so few defenders, or such a
wide array of charges leveled against it. And the charges seem
to have taken. Whether we like to hear it or not, today's
legislatures are located on the outskirts of public esteem and
affection.

This was not always the case. In the formative years of the
republic, legislatures held an exceptionally strong place among

governmental institutions. There were few limitations on the legislature, and constitutions awarded them generous grants of power. The legislatures were at the creative center of state politics.

The decline of the legislature apparently began shortly after the middle of the nineteenth century. Two themes, each an account of legislative devitalization, emerged during this period. One centered in an account of the corruption of legislatures. The arguments were polemical and the charges savage: legislatures were thoroughly dominated by "the interests." Legislators everywhere were in hock. Legislation was bought and sold. Special and local legislation ran riot. Legislatures were the captives of those they sought to regulate. All these allegations easily converged to form the dominant contention that the state legislature was an institution in disarray, an institution that could not and should not be trusted.

The other theme is not so easy to uncover, but it was there. It was an outgrowth of the democratization of American society in the last half of the nineteenth century. Legislatures began to come more and more under the control of the people at large. The legislation that they passed, or that they might pass, was regarded by some men of substance as a threat to their well-being, a threat to established economic institutions, a threat to the economic order as a whole. For those who saw legislative power as menacing, the obvious solution was to set limits on its exercise. And this is precisely what happened. Constitution makers in state after state adopted the theory of the shackled legislature. What may be most remarkable about this is that the theory, the constitutions and the legislatures that resulted survive in about the same form today as they were fashioned then.

Criticism of the legislature is always in vogue. The charges are well known, and not much needs to be said about them. Until *Baker* v. *Carr* and *Reynolds* v. *Sims*, the two main reapportionment cases, a major dilemma of the state legislature was said to be its unrepresentativeness. Urban and suburban areas were being short-changed, ran the complaint, with the result that people were losing confidence in the legislature. This view has always had considerable currency among political scientists. By contrast, the popular journals have usually tended to look for scandal and blight in the legislature. A large number of stories have been published that focus on accounts of "pay-offs," "fetcher bills," "Mae West bills," conflict-of-interest matters, and the like. If we are to believe *The Saturday Evening Post*, *Harper's Magazine*, and other journals, the state legislature is an ethical jungle. Consider the titles of articles with this thrust: "What Those Politicians Do to You" (*The Saturday Evening Post*, 1953); "The Illinois Legislature: A Study in Corruption" (*Harper's Magazine*, 1964); "The State Legislature as a 2-Ring Circus" (*Fact*, 1965); "The Octopus in the State House" (*The Saturday Evening Post*, 1966); and there are many others.

Newspapers have been especially attracted to the idea that the legislative life doesn't amount to much, that the legislature wastes away its time, and that it spends an unusual amount of energy on absurd legislation and hijinks.

In addition, one finds frequently the criticisms that state legislatures are dominated by organized special-interest groups, that legislatures are not responsive to majority preferences either in the electorate or in the institution itself, that legislatures are rarely forces for innovation, that legislative procedures are so complex that it is next to impossible to fix responsibility for decisions taken, that legislative office is not an attractive career for talented men and women—hence, if they do run for the legislature, and get elected, their stay in office is usually brief.

This, then, is the picture of the legislature often presented to the American public. It contains both truth and exaggeration. *Whether the sketch is accurate is perhaps less important than that a great many people appear ready to accept it.* Legislators may see it as more of a caricature of the legislature than any-thing else. Nonetheless, such is the fate of the legislature: It is not only what it makes of itself but what continuing popular interpretation makes of it.

It is against this backdrop—that of massive indictment of the legislative institution—that the objective of strengthening American state legislatures should be discussed. The balance of this paper offers observations on several aspects of the problem: prescriptions or recommendations for reform, the developing interest in the subject, and obstacles to its realization. Finally, the argument will be made that legislative change is predominantly a political problem, that there are no panaceas for legislative ills, and that it is debilitating and maybe even useless to work for the millennium and, in the process, to pass up opportunities for incremental change.

PRESCRIPTIONS

Now to the first of these: prescriptions or recommendations for legislative reform. In the judgment of most political scientists there is no adequate model for an effective legislature. Political scientists, journalists, management organizations, university research agencies, legislators, and legislative auxiliary agencies have advanced an extraordinary number of proposals to change legislative structures and procedures. Sponsors of these ideas are almost as numerous as the ideas themselves.

Legislatures are told that they should increase the legislative term of office; remove the length and subject-matter limitations that govern sessions; reduce the number of committees; equalize their workloads; provide for extensive use of public hearings; revise rules for bill introduction; streamline their processes for budgetary control; introduce computers and data processing; establish better ways for scheduling legislation; use electronic equipment for roll-call voting and other legislative processes; enlarge office space for members; conduct orientation programs for freshman legislators; increase salaries and expense allowances;

add to the number of legislative employees engaged in clerical and research activities; and even eliminate one chamber. And so on and so on.

The proposals are interesting. Some are downright provocative. A few are newsworthy. The proposals have several things in common: 1. all but a few have been offered regularly or intermittently for at least several decades; 2. they are harnessed and trotted out in nearly all the reform articles that appear in the popular journals; and 3. they are all flawed by the same fact, which is that the evidence supporting their worth is not nearly as adequate as it should be.

Recommendations for reform, then, are likely to be troublesome for both the legislator and the academician. They reflect a "credibility gap." No one really knows whether they will do what their sponsors say they will do. No one has said much about the unintended as well as the intended consequences of these changes. No one really knows whether major changes in the state legislative process, in structure or procedures, will make the legislature a better place in which to work, a more nearly equal partner to the governor, a more resourceful institution for the generation of imaginative political ideas. Moreover, although some or all of the reforms mentioned may be good, even excellent, ideas, they are also tired ideas. How do you breathe new life into tired ideas?

What is needed, I think, is a more profound analysis of legislatures. We need to know more about how legislatures actually work. When legislators, political scientists, and others know more about how legislatures maintain themselves and how they satisfy the requirements of their individual members, they will be in a better position to identify the consequences of innovations in the system. No one should expect legislators to take quixotic risks for the sake of tenuous political theory. We need to know what happens when specific changes are introduced. It seems clear that no prescriptions will carry much weight unless they meet functional tests. Reform proposals must be compatible with the real world of legislative functions. No amount of change could take the politics out of the legislative process. No matter how American state legislatures are organized in the last quarter of the twentieth century, they are going to be run by political men for political purposes.

A NEW CONCERN OVER REFORM

In recent years a number of individuals, legislators, groups, and foundations have become concerned over the functioning of American legislatures. Included in these groups are the Eagleton Institute of Politics at Rutgers University, the Citizens Conference on State Legislatures, the National Municipal League, the American Political Science Association, and several foundations. A great deal of private money is being spent on the assumption that legislatures can be changed and revitalized— that they can be strengthened internally and that the states can be strengthened vis-à-vis the federal government.

Important and constructive as these efforts are, they need to be put into perspective. The burgeoning interest in legislatures now notable in foundations, universities, and private groups is helpful, to be sure, but it will not be enough to restore the legislature to the position it once held. The ideas, enthusiasm, and good intentions of a multitude of outsiders are seldom if ever sufficient to reshape major political institutions. What ultimately is required for the continuing welfare of the legislature is a high measure of *diffuse* support among the public for legislatures and the legislative system. To fall back on academic jargon, it can be said that there are two kinds of support that can contribute to the maintenance and vigor of an institution, such as a legislature. One is sometimes called *specific* support. This refers to the support that people give to a political system because they are getting immediate benefits from it. They have a favorable opinion of the system because they are satisfied with its output. Spokesmen for organized labor or organized business may defend the legislature, praise its members, and celebrate its wisdom, because the legislature's policy output specifically meets their demands. But surely no one needs to tell legislators how ephemeral this specific support can be. It is usually short-term. You have it one day, and the next it is gone.

Diffuse support for a political system is more rewarding, more critical to the life of the institution, and much harder to measure. It consists of the steady, day-in, day-out support that people give an institution on the most general of grounds. It is that form of support in which people respect and esteem an institution *not* for its specific output but for its over-all qualities—possibly due to the quality of its members, to the way the institution goes about its business, to its apparent creativity, to its response to changing problems and environments, to its leadership, and so on. Diffuse support sustains an institution because people respect it for what it is, not for what it has done or can do for them. Institutions that enjoy a high measure of diffuse support can withstand all kinds of adversity.

OBSTACLES TO REFORM

There are several specific obstacles to reforming the state legislature that should be considered:

1. In a great many states a leading obstacle to legislative reform is the state constitution itself. The main characteristic of the legislative articles in some state constitutions is a pervasive curb on legislative authority. There are a variety of restrictive provisions, including those that prohibit the legislature from enacting certain kinds of legislation, those that impose detailed requirements concerning legislative procedure, those that settle questions that ordinarily would be treated through legislation. The harshest limitations, it seems obvious, are those that restrict the legislature's control over state finances. There are a good

many state constitutions that establish maximum tax rates, set forth exemptions, and specify uniformity (one effect of which is to prohibit certain kinds of taxes). In a great many states there are limitations on the legislature's authority to incur debt. The practice of earmarking funds, whether by constitution or statute, similarly leads to an erosion of the legislature's fiscal powers. What seems to be the case is that where earmarking is extensive, the legislature's power over the state budget is minimal. The state constitution, with a heavy burden of restrictions on the legislature's fiscal powers, contributes directly to the devitalization of the legislature, to draining its vitality. Legislative autonomy and integrity cannot easily coexist with a constitution that literally shouts that the institution and its members are not to be trusted.

2. In some states, unfortunately, a leading obstacle to legislative reform has been the governor. The fact that the governor does not express open opposition to reform is not really the test. It is rather a case of the governor doing little or nothing to facilitate it. He can always claim that reform of the legislature is "the legislature's business." The truth of the matter is that the strengthening of any branch of government is a matter for all of government. Why governors should be indifferent to legislative reform is not hard to explain. As things stand now, there are few legislatures that have achieved parity with the governor. The typical governor is likely to believe that a weak legislature is likely to serve his interests better. There is no doubt but that he has most of the advantages today. He has superior visibility, superior constitutional position, superior staff assistance, superior position in the state party organization, superior access to political resources (jobs, publicity, prestige, information, and so on), and perhaps a superior claim to represent statewide interests. The general pattern in the states is one of gubernatorial leadership and legislative subordination. Governors have always found it fairly easy to convince legislatures that the legislatures should help them reform or streamline the administra-

tive branch. But it is a rare governor who has contributed any energy or initiative to matters of strengthening the legislature.

3. A third obstacle to legislative reform is the legislature itself; more specifically, it is the members: the leadership *and* the rank-and-file. Reform is scarcely ever neutral. Institutional change is likely to manifest itself in a somewhat new distribution of power. After changes are made, some members are going to have more power than before and others are going to have less power. As Alan Rosenthal has pointed out, if a decision is taken to strengthen the party caucus by giving it expert staff assistance, the legislative party organization will gain advantage, perhaps at the expense of the individual member, perhaps at the expense of the committee system. If committees are strengthened by the addition of staff assistance, the legislative leadership in some measure is likely to be weakened. If legislative leaders are given professional staff, the effect may be to cut into committee power and independence. It is very difficult to know precisely what effects may result from changes in the institution. The point, in any case, is a simple one: Some legislative leaders and some rank-and-file members are likely to be chary of change because they think that they will be worse off in power terms if change is made.

4. A fourth obstacle to legislative reform is partisanship. If reform proposals are dramatized as the inspiration of simply one party, they run a good risk of becoming tainted, of being categorized as a partisan grab for power. In states where there is two-party competition, it seems far more likely that the press, organized interests, and the attentive citizenry will view reform sympathetically if they see both parties as sponsors of it.

There are a host of miscellaneous reasons why reform is difficult to bring about: The public often seems to be as indifferent to legislative improvement as it is to the legislature itself. Few interest groups see any stake in reform; indeed, it may be that most fear it because of its consequences for the distribution of power within the legislature. A large number of legislators have remarkably short legislative careers; they move in and out of the legislature as if in a game of musical chairs, seldom pausing to reflect on the legislature *qua* legislature. The party organizations within the districts or even statewide seldom express much interest in the matter, preferring, it seems, to concentrate on the legislature as a transmission belt for conveying party advantages. If indifference to the legislature could be assembled, put into units, and laid out, it would stretch easily from Augusta, Maine to Austin, Texas; from Olympia, Washington to Tallahassee, Florida; from Jackson, Mississippi, to Bismarck, North Dakota. *That, in my judgment, is the dominant truth to be known about legislative reform—that only a few people at any one time really care about it, despite its massive significance for the vitality of democratic government.*

THE POLITICAL PROBLEM

Bold recommendations for strengthening popular support for the state legislature are not easily uncovered. No "model" for an "effective" legislature exists. But there are several considerations that should be kept in mind. Under ordinary circumstances the help that outsiders can give to upgrading the legislature, or to strengthening its position with the public, will be modest. They can help to identify problems. They can help to generate solutions. They can provide general public instruction. Sometimes they can rally the attentive public to use its political resources. When they do these things, they help to support reform-minded legislators. Nonetheless, the over-all contribution they can make is limited. When all is said and done, they are still outsiders.

This observation leads to a second point: A major share of the energy and resourcefulness required to strengthen state legislatures must come from legislators themselves. They, better than anyone else, know what it is all about, know what the stakes are, know where opportunities exist, know what is feasible and what is not, and know how legislative careers are going to be affected by legislative processes.

A third point is this: The main burden of reinvigorating the legislature, hopefully giving it parity with the governor, lies with the leaders of the legislatures. Democratic theory exaggerates the willingness and ability of the people, or of the rank-and-file members of any institution, to govern themselves. In similar fashion, democratic theory seems to diminish the role of leadership. The evidence suggests that the wider public cannot be involved, except in indirect ways, with questions of legislative change. For one reason, the public is preoccupied with other things. And second, it is apparent that the public can understand policy much better than it can understand structure, function, and process.

Put together and slightly expanded, the argument of this paper is as follows: 1. the public as a whole cannot be expected to implicate itself seriously in matters of legislative change; 2. interested outsiders are limited in what they can do; 3. governors can hardly be expected to lie awake nights thinking of ways by which the legislature can win greater independence and power; 4. political interest groups that like the legislature the way it is are not going to be impatient advocates of experimentation; and 5. the press is simply unpredictable. The press lives by exaggeration. There are some grounds for believing that the press would rather have an exciting issue to report than major, though quiet, accomplishment. And so it goes—in matters of legislative reform, the legislature is much more on its own than is usually recognized.

Change in political institutions comes hard. Old arrangements hang on and on. Conventional ways of doing things have a momentum of their own, quite apart from the men who use them. To bring about change in established institutions requires exceptional tenacity on the part of the leadership. It requires skills of a high order—skills in bargaining, in weighing costs and gains, in identifying alternatives, in assessing feasibility, in balancing interests, in placating the disenchanted.

Strengthening the legislature is first and foremost a political problem. For this special problem, legislative leaders have more political resources than anyone else. This is why the main burden rests on them. What they elect to do, or are pressured into doing, will determine how the legislature looks, how it goes about its business, and how significant a role it plays in the political system.

Legislative Reform and the Legislative Leader

CHARLES O. DAVIS

In facing the question of its own reform, the legislature occupies the peculiar position of being at once the object of the exercise and the engine of its accomplishment. What gets done, finally, must be done by the legislature, upon itself.

Others may prescribe; and the prescriptions may be, and usually are, quite well targeted to what the observer can readily identify as inefficient processes. But having prescribed, the observer is impotent. The doctor who prescribes and observes a lack of progress can always take direct action, including surgery. Political scientists, or citizen organizations, having prescribed, can do little more than observe, cheer, lament, groan, attempt to rally public opinion or, in the most desperate of circumstance, actually run for office and work within the institution. Newspapers may, and often do, rage at the failures of legislatures. These failures are almost always the ones that do not meet the agenda for government set by the newspaper. Most newspapers have an abysmal understanding of what a legislature really is, and therefore their prescriptions most often fall on deaf ears, or are unworkable even if desirable. For many other reasons, all kinds of citizens who feel strongly about legislative reform are inhibited from accomplishment because they don't belong to the legislature.

The legislature, usually, takes a serious view of reform proposals. The view may be completely hostile, but it is not indifferent. The legislature is, after all, a sensitive organism that quickly reacts to any form of attack, either against it as a body or against its members as legislators. Members of the legislature usually feel that those who are not in do not understand what being in is. They are often demonstrably right in this belief, and each time they are right their resistance to change hardens a little bit.

Legislators are also quite busy with other things; as a matter of fact, the most intense pressure for reform of the legislature almost always arises precisely at the time when the legislature is most occupied with agonizing problems, and this is not by coincidence. It supports the conclusion that visibility of the legislature, above all else, is the condition that fertilizes reform. When the legislature has gone home, and becomes once again the invisible branch of government, the cry for its reform diminishes to an occasional whisper.

None of this is to say that reform, or modernization, or improvement, or whatever it may be called, is not desirable and is not feasible. It is both, and knowledgeable legislative leaders recognize its necessity. What they do object to, and what arouses their frequent concern, is uninformed and uneducated reaction—the kind that demonstrates ignorance of the body and its purposes.

LEGISLATURES AND THEIR LEADERSHIP

The vision of reform held by the leadership is crucial to accomplishment. In state after state, it has been demonstrated that, without the involvement or at least the acquiescence of the leadership, there will be no reform of the legislature.

Perhaps it is instructive to consider just what the legislative leadership is, if one is to accept the fact of its overwhelming importance in reform. And in this process of definition, it is probably appropriate first to make certain that there is some understanding of what the legislature itself is; for lack of understanding of the legislature itself leads more do-gooders and well-wishers to defeat than is generally acknowledged.

The legislature is a body of people, and realization of that is the beginning of understanding. It is not a single-minded executive; it is not a reflective judiciary. It cannot retire to chambers or behind doors to judge, reflect, or proclaim. It is a cockpit, an arena in which the interests of all the people of the state meet and clash, in the open and before all the rest of the state. The men and women of the legislature have in mind those interests—some parochial, some vertical, some horizontal. But it is the accommodation of those interests that drives the legislature; and accommodation in public is not, and never will be, a piece of beautiful art.

The governor, relying on staff aides who work in anonymity, may issue Olympian statements of utter clarity, apparently completely free of debate, wrangle, partisanship, and the clash of interest. It all went on behind closed doors in the governor's office; nobody saw it, and the governor's statement may be majestic in tone but stupid in content.

This the legislature can hardly do. Solution—real solution of problems—seldom happens in government, and it is in the legislature, where the traffic ebbs and flows, and where passions run high and open, that the settlements and accommodations are made that are the real stuff of government.

The leadership of this legislature is composed of its leaders, and when one tries to get beyond that rather nonsensical definition, trouble always arises. For the fact is that there is titular leadership in a legislature, and there is real leadership. More

often than not, fortunately, the two coincide in the same individuals. The Speaker and his floor leaders usually constitute
the officially recognized leadership of the House. But in many
states—and particularly those that practice rotating leadership—
the real power may lie with a clique or circle whose members
may or may not carry title. In the Senate this situation is often
more confused by the role of the lieutenant governor, who
may or may not be a real leader in that body.

All of this, of course, is more confusing and more confounding
to those on the outside than it is to the members, who have
a very real understanding—attained very quickly—of where the
power lies. And so long as they understand it, and can deal
effectively with it, the system moves along quite satisfactorily
for all who serve within it.

Our particular concern is not with the who of leadership,
or the definition by title. What we are here concerned with is
the use by the legislative leader of his power to improve his
legislature. Let us for a moment look at that general goal, variously called improvement, modernization, reform, etc. Let us
then look at the leader's stake and role in it, and finally at
some of the resources available to him.

Many definitions of a model legislature exist, and probably
most legislators have some kind of a vision of their own of
what that model might be, including some who are perfectly
satisfied with what they have. There are problems involved in
producing a neat definition of legislative improvement. But if
one looks at the other end of the road—at what he would like
to see the legislature be able to do—he comes more quickly
to his model, because what the legislature ought to be able
to do is to cope absolutely, completely, and independently with
any issue within the total framework of state government.

The model legislature ought to be fiercely independent—not
that its members alone can cope with everything, but that it
has the resources, or knows how to obtain the resources, to cope.
It will not be subservient to the governor, to the administrative

agencies, to the press, or to anyone else. It may or may not co-operate with those institutions, but the choice is its own, and it is prepared for the consequences of its actions. All of this means, of course, that above everything else the legislature must have knowledge. It must have access to information, it must have the ability to gather and interpret information, it must be able to arrive at judgments after consideration of alternatives, and it must have the knowledge to defend its choice.

Thus we come around to the needs of a reformed legislature —staff, quarters, compensation, facilities, unfettered constitutional rights, equipment, organization, and so forth. They have all been discussed, written about, and lectured upon for some years now, and we shall continue to talk of them for a good while to come. It is the nitty-gritty of reform, and the legislator must consider all of these tools and techniques in the light of his own needs and the needs imposed by the governance of his state.

But I submit that the beginning of truth in this area of reform lies in first knowing what the final objective is—what the reformed legislature is going to be able to do once it is reformed. From that understanding, one moves to the techniques and the details.

LEADERSHIP STAKES IN REFORM

All of this, of course, has profound implications for the legislative leader. Traditionally, many leaders have resisted reform, although that breed is becoming rarer and rarer. To that leader, power was something to hoard, and since knowledge is power, knowledge, too, was something to hoard. The duty of the membership was to follow the leadership's line, and the fewer resources the membership had with which to try to understand that line, the more likely the leader was to have his undisputed way.

Usually, his loyalty was to his governor, although in some

cases the reverse was true. And if his party did not hold the governorship, then his loyalty might be to his party, or to his small circle of comrades, or simply to himself. But the idea of belonging to the *legislature* and being, first and above all, a *legislator*, didn't figure in his operation. It was a neat, tidy arrangement. The governor budgeted the state; the legislature made the necessary accommodations with the special interests and the political brokers, took care of a few bills that individual members needed for a variety of reasons, drew its few hundred dollars, and went home. Nobody in the legislature, except the leadership, quite knew what had happened; the press and the intellectual community thought "governor" and "government" were synonymous; and a few leaders enjoyed the prerogatives of power, albeit anonymously.

Of course, the stress and strain of mid-twentieth-century life proved to be too much for this rather pastoral approach, and in more and more states, enlightened legislators, newspapermen, and academics opened the way to a more effective legislative arrangement.

We are often asked why the legislative leader should support reform, given the reasonable chance that in the end he will dilute his previously undisputed power. I have heard many of the old-timers deride the concept, and I have heard many of the new breed describe their motives, and while much of it is personal in nature, relating to the individual, there are some common threads running through the conversations.

In the first place, a number of legislative leaders work to achieve a more enlightened legislature simply because it is right; simply because they believe in the federal system of government, the sovereignty of the states, and the co-equal status of the legislature. And more public officials than are ever given credit for it are public officials because they want to do things right.

Second, under the stresses of the fearful complexity of our lives today, the legislature cannot exist in the half life of incompetence. The legislative leader alone cannot compete with the executive and the agencies; he must have staff resources, and he must be able to deal with a reasonably well-informed body of members. Leader after leader has found beyond question that his real power in state government becomes much greater when he stands at the head of a body of reasonable, knowledgeable, responsible legislators, as opposed to being the chieftain of an ignorant tribe whom nobody respects.

Third, in order to get the resources he needs, he must give something to the members who support him, and this leads to all kinds of new accommodations within the legislature. For one thing, the minority's rights must be protected and its access to information must be provided. No legislature moves into a position of effectiveness unless the effort is essentially bipartisan. But in providing more services to his members, the leader finds he has not given up power at all, but has built understanding and a stronger power base. He deals fairly with his members and effectively with the outside world, and most legislators can do nothing but applaud that.

The simple fact is that today, a legislative leader alone cannot deal effectively with the governor, the press, or the special interests in his state. If he is alone, operating as an individual, he is a loser before the fray begins, because he just cannot possibly know as much as his adversaries, and very likely the only information he has is what they give him. He can neither deal with them nor counter their strategies, and he becomes a leader in name only. On the other hand, the leader of a body that has its independent research, its independent sources of information, that has respect for itself, that has enough efficiency of process so that it knows where it is going as well as where it has been—the leader of that kind of a body meets the governor and everyone else on equal terms. Not that state government should be thought of only as a battlefield; but our government is based on a clash of ideas, and the more nearly equal the adversaries, the more likely it is that good government will result.

AVAILABLE RESOURCES

The case for the leader's stake in an effective legislature can be made rather effectively, and has in fact been made in state after state. The real question today for most legislative leaders is not "Why?" but "How?" That, of course, is the reason for the growing number of seminars being held for legislators and their leadership. Thus one of the resources available to the leader today is the meeting—an increasing number of which are concerned with this subject. This leader-to-leader contact is one of the prime purposes of the National Conference of State Legislative Leaders, and it is by providing settings, both in small meetings and large, that the National Conference becomes a resource for the leader who needs to know more about reform. It is unique among all the organizations of government in that it is exclusively of and for the leadership, and the point of view of the organization is the point of view of the leader.

We have long recognized our need for the resources of two other great bodies of society: the citizen and the academic. Academic resources are well known to most legislative leaders, although not so well used, I suspect, as they should be. We have been fortunate in the National Conference to have established such a firm relationship with the Eagleton Institute of Politics at Rutgers University. Although it is certainly not the only academic institution capable of providing resource backup to the leader, it is uniquely concerned with state government and the politics of state government. And it is more sensitive than most institutions to the problems and the techniques of legislative reform. Not only through the National Conference, for which it serves as the research arm, but as an independent source, Eagleton is available to every legislative leader who can use its background of experience, knowledge, and information. Eagleton studies of legislatures in a growing number of states provide an important body of knowledge in this field. Every leader should at least consider the possibility of such a study of his own legislature.

Of course, every leader is aware that resources are available to him from the citizen sector. The trouble usually is that they are too available, too vocal, and either impractical or unpolitical, or both. Not so with the Citizens Conference on State Legislatures, which has become in the period of a few years a prime source of information and technique for any leader who is pushing ahead. I seriously doubt if there is any important legislative reform movement afoot in this country about which the Citizens Conference is not aware and in which it has not been involved to some extent.

Thus the legislative leader who sees his stake in reform, and decides to push along from where he is now, no matter where that may be, to where he thinks he ought to be, no matter where that is—that leader has resources available, and he should tap them. He has the experience of other leaders in other states, which he can get through legislator organizations such as the National Conference. He has the academic community, growing more and more aware of the importance of an effective legislature. And he has knowledgeable and capable citizen organizations to help smooth his path, to provide information, and to rally public opinion to his side. He need not, in other words, try to invent the wheel all over again. He is not alone.

CONCLUSION

The most satisfactory definition I have of the legislative leader is that he, unlike his colleagues on the benches, always sees tomorrow. The membership by and large is concerned with today, and the problems of today, but the leader sees tomorrow, and all the tomorrows to come. He has a vision of where he wants to lead or to drive this body of men and women; he knows why he wants to get them there; he knows what he is going to do with them when he does; and finally and most hopefully, he knows how to do it, or, being a leader, he knows where to find out how to do it.

The Constitutional Convention as a Device for Legislative Change

HOWARD PENNIMAN

The subject matter of this essay was suggested early in the spring of 1968 when nearly all observers believed that Maryland would soon adopt a good constitution written by a generally excellent convention that included experienced public servants, respected civic leaders, and able scholars. The constitution, which had been widely acclaimed in the national press as "the finest state constitution in the nation" and "a model for other states to follow," seemed certain of ratification if only the electorate turned out in large enough numbers. A big vote, it was said, would ensure victory against the efforts of special interests.

THE DEFEAT OF A CONSTITUTION

The campaign for ratification was well-financed and generally well-manned. The opposition was made up of some county courthouse crowds in the hinterlands whose positions were jeopardized by the new document, a precious few respected citizens (two of seven members of the Court of Appeals being the most obvious ones), a handful of archconservatives who had opposed calling the constitutional convention in the first place, a ragtag group of leaders of district machines in a couple of sections of Baltimore, and a full quota of just plain political misfits. Arrayed against this unappetizing crew were nearly all the respectable leaders of the state. Vigorously supporting the ratification of the new constitution were both U.S. senators, Governor Spiro T. Agnew, and the two living ex-governors of the state (former Governor J. Millard Tawes was still perhaps the most potent organization man in the state; he had initiated the efforts for the new constitution and had been a delegate and honorary president of the convention), seven of the eight members of Congress from Maryland, the mayor of Baltimore (who had just been elected by a four-to-one margin), the leaders of both parties in both houses of the Maryland General Assembly, every important state business group, the trade unions, and all daily papers in the state plus the three Washington, D.C., papers that service two of the three most populous counties in Maryland.

The voters came out in numbers far greater than in the preceding spring when convention delegates had been elected by less than 20 percent of the state's electorate. Just under 50 percent of them cast their ballots on May 14, 1968, and they overwhelmingly turned down the new document. Only the two Washington suburban counties favored it. The fifty-three-thousand-vote margin piled up in the suburban counties was quickly erased, and the final margin against the constitution was more than eighty-three thousand out of a vote of 650,000.

The defeat in Maryland marked the fourth state constitution to be rejected in a period of less than five years. The constitutions of Kentucky, Rhode Island, and New York had preceded the Maryland document in defeat. The last constitution written by a convention and approved by the people was that of Michigan, and its adoption in 1963 may well have been a fluke. Professor Warren Miller of the University of Michigan has said that the United Automobile Workers, who opposed the constitution, commissioned an opinion survey to discover what the Michigan voters thought about the proposed constitution. The survey findings indicated that the voters strongly supported the document. The U.A.W. was advised that even a major campaign would not be enough to alter the outcome. The constitution was approved by the narrow margin of 810,180 to 799,420 votes. One can only guess what would have happened if the union had made an all-out effort to defeat the constitution.

For reasons that we will discuss later, then, the constitutional convention may be of limited value as a device for reforming the state legislature. Slightly more promising may be the piecemeal amendment of an existing constitution. Here, the cases of Pennsylvania and Virginia may be instructive. The constitutional convention is, or at least can be, an excellent device for writing legislative reform. None of the recently defeated constitutions was injured seriously, if at all, by provisions relating to the legislatures. And most of the documents included significant provisions for modernizing the legislatures. The constitutions, and therefore the legislative reforms, were destroyed by opposition that accumulated around other provisions. In New York, for example, many leading citizens, reform organizations, and newspapers (including the New York *Times*) questioned the wisdom of approving the proposed constitution. The opposition centered around the Blaine amendment repeal and the subsequent exacerbation of religious cleavages in the state. In New York, too, the enabling act itself had built deep and bitter partisan divisions into the convention and so into the constitution.

THE CONVENTION PROCESS

In Maryland, the legislature guarded against excessive partisanship by calling for nonpartisan elections of convention delegates.

In some areas—notably in the Washington suburbs and in some sections of Baltimore County—local party leaders did their share to prevent unnecessary conflict by jointly selecting and backing bipartisan slates that easily won election in most districts. The convention itself was so careful to exclude partisanship that there was never a caucus of either the Democrats or the Republicans, and it was well into the session before newspaper reporters identified the labels of all the participants. Indeed, the convention was so nonpartisan in character that 108 Democrats agreed with the handful of Republicans to create a redistricting commission appointed equally by the majority and minority leaders of the two houses. The odd man and chairman would be appointed by the governor. In spite of the fact that this arrangement then appeared to mean that the first commission in 1970 would have a Republican majority, no question was raised on that matter either in committee or on the floor of the convention.

In Maryland, also, the delegates had learned from the conflict over the religious issue in New York. The Roman Catholic Archdiocese of Baltimore refused to allow clerics to campaign for convention seats. (A Methodist minister was elected from Baltimore, but his presence was in no way divisive.) The convention itself avoided all religious debates of consequence. Early in the session it adopted a provision in the declaration of rights that was nearly identical with the provision in the First Amendment of the national Constitution, on the sensible ground that the U. S. Supreme Court was going to interpret the actions of the state in terms of the provisions of the First and Fourteenth Amendments in any case. There were no other serious debates involving religion during the whole session.

Maryland, then, avoided the most obvious difficulties of the New York convention. Its proposed constitution was not defeated by a two-and-a-half-to-one margin as in New York, but the lesser margin was hardly comforting. Religion and party did not defeat the reform, but other unforeseen issues did.

Before turning to the defeat of the constitution and an

estimate of the problems in constitutional ratification, let us first take a quick look at the kind of legislative reform that the proposed constitution would have provided. The constitution would have: 1. reduced the size of both houses of the Maryland General Assembly; 2. assured equal representation of citizens by moving to single-member districts and away from the multi-member districts that had allowed district majorities to exclude minorities from all representation; 3. extended the length of the sessions; 4. increased legislative salaries; 5. increased the powers of the legislature; and 6. removed the need to enact detailed local legislation.

The legislative article was the product of a convention committee that included among its members some key figures in the legislature, but which had a majority of nonmembers. Nearly every important current or recent member of both houses testified at the committee hearings. The liaison committee of the Maryland General Assembly was carefully consulted. The final product was perhaps not what the more conservative legislative members might have wished, but few of them were bitterly opposed, and most legislators warmly favored the committee's recommendations. No significant changes were made in the committee's proposals on the floor of the convention. The size of each house of the legislature was increased beyond the recommendations of the committee, but not by much. Other provisions remained largely as reported to the floor.

Neither the committee nor the convention adopted any far-out changes in the traditional legislative pattern. There were attempts to create a unicameral body, but these were decisively beaten in committee and on the floor.

Debate was sometimes sharp on the floor with respect to the size of the legislature, the single-member district system, and the date of the first redistricting. There was some bitterness among the losers over each of these issues, but the majorities supporting the convention decisions were large and the minorities seemed to swallow their unhappiness with good grace as the session wore on. The delegates recognized that a reduction in the size of the legislature would increase slightly the number of counties that would be without their own representative in 1970, but they recognized also that ultimately this change had to come because some counties are rapidly increasing in population while others are continuing to lose citizens. Delegates also recognized that the courts would force an early redistricting even if the constitution did not require it. They were aware that this debate had been for the record. Only the single-member versus multimember district fight had real substance. The outcome would affect the power of some of the small-time Baltimore district bosses, and they were bitterly opposed. Their later effort to defeat the constitution was the only opposition that perhaps might be directly traced to the legislative provision. Often as not, however, they cited other matters as their grounds for opposition.

THE NATURE OF OPPOSITION

In the debate that followed the convention's action, opponents concentrated on a few themes. They noted the increased power in the hands of the governor and the abolition of constitutional status for the clerks of court, the sheriff, and the registrars of wills. They argued that democratic government was certain to be weakened with the decrease in the number of persons popularly elected, the centralization of the court system, the increased salaries of state officials, and the danger of regional governments.

The major efforts of the opponents, however, were concentrated on essentially fictitious issues. They charged that the new government would cost millions more in taxes every year. Their earliest estimate was 153 million dollars, which was later discarded when it was pointed out that the state would have to build new courthouses in every county each year to justify that figure. But the fear of higher costs and new taxes was never dispelled, in spite of careful studies that suggested there would be no increased cost after the two-year transition period.

Race was the second major fictitious issue constantly before the people of the state. In the Washington suburban area opponents raised the specter of masses of blacks invading the suburbs on election day. Black leader Julius Hobson, they said, would bus the blacks into Prince Georges and Montgomery Counties to vote in state and local elections if the new constitution were ratified. In the counties surrounding Baltimore city the race issue was raised differently. Here it was said that the city of Baltimore would be able to annex the neighboring counties by unilateral action. Since a large number of the residents of the counties moved from Baltimore city precisely because they had wanted to escape the increasing number of blacks in the central city, they were hardly prepared to accept black domination under the new constitution. In the city of Baltimore, where small machines dominate the politics of some legislative districts, sound trucks moved up and down the streets on the weekend before the election asserting that the old constitution meant "white power." A massive 80.6 percent of the voters in those districts cast their votes against the constitution.

Professor Robert D. Loevy, then associate director of the field politics center of Goucher College, has provided some interesting figures on the voting in the special constitutional election as compared with some earlier elections. Most of his figures are for the metropolitan areas around Washington and Baltimore. These two areas include about four-fifths of the population of the state. By and large, they are urban, but some partially rural counties are included in these metropolitan areas. He has broken down the census tracts so as to provide generally accurate demographic data for his precincts.

He found that education and income were closely related to the vote for the constitution. These figures show that precincts where a majority of the voters were college-educated went solidly for the constitution, at a rate of 68 to 32 percent. The precincts of lesser educational levels voted against the constitution. Two exceptions were the only precincts where the majority of voters had finished the sixth grade or less. These two were black precincts, and backed the constitution 72 to 28 percent. The figures for income show comparable results. The very poor precincts (black) backed the constitution, as did the well-to-do precincts. In both types of precincts clear majorities voted in favor. Districts that were lower in income but not poor and where annual incomes ranged from five thousand to seven thousand dollars were different. They voted two-to-one to reject the constitution. Professor Loevy notes that the same trend was to be found in Montgomery and Prince Georges Counties as elsewhere in the state, but that in the Washington suburban counties a majority of the people in all types of precincts favored the constitution. In Montgomery County even the five-thousand-to-seven-thousand-dollar-income precincts backed it by 59.2 percent, while the wealthier precincts, with average incomes above nine thousand dollars, gave 73.8 percent of their votes for the document. The figures in Prince Georges are not quite so impressive, but they are closer to the Montgomery County figures than to those of the state as a whole.

When he looked at past voting behavior, Loevy came up with equally interesting data. He found that precincts that had generally voted Republican were more likely to have supported the constitution. By contrast, in those that had voted consistently Democratic, only one out of five voters favored the constitution. Loevy also compared the precinct votes in the Democratic gubernatorial primary in 1966 with the vote for and against the constitution. The Democrats in 1966 nominated archconservative George P. Mahoney by a very narrow margin over liberal Congressman Carlton R. Sickles and organization-supported Thomas Finan. Mahoney ran on the slogan, "Your home is your castle," and opposed all open-housing legislation. In precincts that had supported Mahoney, about 75 percent voted against the constitution; in those which had gone for Finan, the vote was equally divided; and in those where Sickles had won, the constitution received about 70 percent of the vote.

Incidentally, Loevy's data show also that in precincts where the Wallace vote in 1964 was less than 10 percent, the support for the constitution reached 71.5 percent. By contrast, in the 187 precincts where Wallace received 70 percent or more of the vote, support of the constitution fell to a mere 18.5 percent, while the opposition swelled to 81.5 percent.

These figures again point up the fact that persons who support liberal candidates in national elections may often cast very conservative votes in state and local elections and even in presidential primaries. This is particularly true if the issues are presented to them in terms of race or higher taxes. The Michigan Survey Research Center has pointed out that there is very little positive connection between support of liberal national candidates and social welfare legislation on the one hand and support of such things as civil liberties and civil rights on the other. Robert Agger and others have noted that those who have consistently supported liberal candidates on the national level may oppose measures to improve schools, parks, and even garbage collection at the local level, if they think that these reforms will increase their taxes. A glance at the presidential primary election returns in Gary, Indiana and sections of Maryland in 1964 and at the later general election vote in the same areas make clear the gap between support of social welfare measures and civil rights. Although both areas supported the Johnson-Humphrey ticket in November, both gave Wallace heavy support in the primary to demonstrate their opposition to civil rights.

CONCLUSION

Whole constitutions offered to the voters for their approval obviously can be sandbagged by negative votes cast on largely irrelevant issues that have touched the very tender nerves of a great many voters. The Maryland election brought out hundreds of thousands of worried citizens who wished to vote against that which was not going to happen anyway. Many of these voters never considered the issues of governmental organization and structure. They voted only their fears, and the consequences were devastating for reform.

At the turn of the century, major changes were made in the government and politics of the states—particularly those in the Middle and Far West. New constitutions were adopted in a number of these states. The constitutions were accepted by the voters because their fears of the present and their hopes for the future dictated change. Farmers who supported the great constitutional reforms of the late nineteenth and early twentieth centuries were men who feared the continuation of what they thought to be the political and economic domination by the railroads, the eastern banks, and their political lackeys. They hoped to gain political independence and economic improvement through the changes.

In Maryland in 1968 many working-class and lower-middle-class white voters feared that change would cause them to lose their increasing economic well-being to high taxes and their new-found social status to integration. They outnumbered the well-off whites who wanted "better government," and the blacks, who were much like the supporters of reform in the earlier era. The blacks saw in the new constitution the chance for economic progress and for more equitable political representation. In the 127 all-black precincts in Baltimore the vote favoring the constitution averaged 82.3 percent. The turnout, however, was not heavy in these precincts.

Out of the debacle of the recent constitutional conventions may come some reforms that can be adopted by the normal amendment processes. There is now some hope for minor legislative reform in Maryland. Sessions of the legislature may be lengthened and salaries increased, but little else in the way of legislative reform seemed likely two years after the defeat of the constitution.

At this time in our state constitutional histories, the piecemeal process chosen by Pennsylvania and Virginia may be the road to reform. In any case, it deserves very careful consideration. It does not force the voters into an all-or-nothing choice, and it does not allow the accumulation of grievances that helped destroy the efforts in New York, Kentucky, Rhode Island, and Maryland. Students of Pennsylvania government may not be impressed by the changes made by legislature-sponsored amendments or by a state convention of limited jurisdiction. Nevertheless, a considerable number of amendments to modernize the government have been adopted. Some of those changes still have not been made in the four states that depended entirely upon their conventions for constitutional revision.

The Illinois Experience in Legislative Modernization

HAROLD A. KATZ

We are in a period in our history when many legislators, citizens, and academicians are taking a fresh look at what has been called the fountainhead of American democracy—the state legislatures in the United States. In Illinois, under the leadership of a legislative commission, we have been engaged for almost two years in this task, and once begun, it is a never-ending quest. At the outset let me dispel any illusion that any of us think that a program for modernization and reorganization is an exportable, packaged commodity. On the contrary, a workable program must grow out of local conditions and circumstances. However, because an actual case experience may provide some perspective for other states, I shall describe what has been done in Illinois.

CONDITIONS IN THE LEGISLATURE

Our legislature has been beset by some fairly typical problems. We have probably dealt with our problems no better nor any worse than most. Our state is a large and prosperous one, but suffice it to say that the prosperity has never reflected itself in the facilities provided within the legislative branch. Members of the House of Representatives, in which I serve, have no offices in which to work or to see constituents. You have perhaps heard of the sign once posted in a western legislature that read: "Senators who don't have a secretary of their own can take advantage of the girls in the steno pool." We in the House have never had secretaries of our own, or personal staff for aid in research on the enormous number of bills that come before us. I am persuaded, however, that the one that gets taken advantage of in a situation such as this is the public. Quite often the private interests prevail over the public interest, as groups with particular ends to further fill the vacuum created by the absence of adequate legislative facilities and staff. Knowledgeable lobbyists armed with selected statistics are extremely persuasive with overly busy, understaffed legislators.

In Illinois, the end of the session logjam has become notorious. Both parties hold back approval of bills hoping for political advantage from the confusion and hoping to make last-minute deals.

One item, however, tells volumes about the extent of the confusion that has accompanied the closing days of the session in Illinois. The 1965 session of our legislature extended over a six-month period. We passed 2211 bills in all. Of these, 1363 bills, or 61 percent, passed in the final week of the session. One of the bills that ostensibly passed was one to double the mileage allowance of legislators. It was only after the governor had signed the bill that someone discovered that the Senate had neglected to vote upon it. The governor hastily withdrew his signature. When things are happening so fast in the legislature that legislators inadvertently fail to vote upon a bill that will result in an increase in their own mileage allowance, some improvements in the way the public's business is being conducted are obviously in order.

THE ILLINOIS COMMISSION AND ITS WORK

The legislative modernization program began with the introduction at the 1965 session of our legislature of a bill, with
broad bipartisan support, creating a commission to study the
processes and operations of the Illinois General Assembly. At
that time, our Senate was under Republican control and our
House had a Democratic majority. The Illinois Commission on the
Organization of the General Assembly consisted of twenty members, plus two *ex officio* members, the Speaker of the House, and
the president pro tem of the Senate. There were three members
from the majority party and two from the minority from each
chamber. Provided also were ten public members, but unlike the
usual appointment procedure in Illinois, the public members were
to be appointed by the legislative leaders rather than by the
governor. The commission to reorganize the legislative branch was
thus wholly under the control of the legislature. At the same
time, neither party enjoyed a numerical advantage on the commission, and recommendations and decisions had to result from
persuasion and consensus rather than party loyalty.

Several additional provisions in the bill proved to be particularly
useful. One required our state universities and colleges to co-
operate with the commission; we subsequently received much
assistance from the faculty members of the state universities.
Also invited, at our request, were experts in various fields such
as appropriations and legislative rules and procedures, who
served as consultants to our commission and taught at the college
campuses at the same time. Private universities in the state also
were generous with their consulting services. For example, the
computer center at Northwestern University indexed the public
testimony presented before the commission. The bill appropriated
thirty thousand dollars for the study, but permitted the com-

mission to accept gifts or grants to further its work. We secured a federal tax-exempt status and received from Illinois foundations and companies an additional 13,300 dollars, which has proved most helpful in the furthering of our work.

We divided the subject matter into the following areas of inquiry: 1. constitutional impacts on the legislative process; 2. general legislative procedures and techniques; 3. direct legislative facilities and services; 4. committees and commissions; 5. legislative publications, enrolling and engrossing, and utilization of data processing; 6. the appropriations process; and 7. legislative service agencies.

For each area of study, a subcommittee was established that included at its head a commission member, appointed by the chairman without regard to party, and a professional consultant knowledgeable in the particular field. The commission as a whole held public hearings to which legislators and other public officials, scholars, and other interested persons, organizations, and the lobbying groups were invited to present testimony. The testimony was then indexed by computer, and the comments and suggestions broken down by subject matter and referred to the appropriate subcommittees for consideration. Each subcommittee then developed a tentative set of recommendations. These were presented as trial balloons for discussion by all commission members, and a small group of other legislators, academicians, and selected citizens, at an informal three-day conference arranged by the University of Illinois. Following the conference, the recommendations were reconsidered by the particular subcommittees and then by the full commission; a tentative report was drafted and submitted to all members. There followed a three-day conference of all commission members, where there was a full consideration of the final recommendations and of the language of the proposed report. The final draft of the report was submitted to each member, and an opportunity afforded to dissent from particular recommendations. The publication was then rushed, so that the final report could be in the hands of each member by the opening day of the session.

The Illinois Commission on the Organization of the General Assembly made a total of eighty-seven recommendations for improvements in the legislative operation, of which eighty-four represented unanimous recommendations. Among the recommendations were:

1. Reduction in the number of committees and continuance of the major ones between the sessions as joint interim committees with full-time majority-minority professional staffing.

2. Increased "due process" in legislative procedures, to provide improved provisions for notice to members and to the public and full opportunity to be informed and to be heard.

3. A legislative procedures schedule and timetable to minimize the end-of-the-session logjam.

4. The absolute right of a minority to verification of a roll call, which is extremely important, particularly in a state that utilizes electronic voting.

5. A major overhaul of the appropriations process and legislative responsibility for budget-making procedures. It was difficult to avoid the conclusion from our study that the Illinois General Assembly had withdrawn from meaningful participation in the appropriations process.

6. A major change in legislative printing, including the use of offset instead of letterpress for printing of bills and amendments. We concluded that the existing system was costly and inefficient; it required unnecessary typing and printing; its final products were clumsy to use in contrast to a system that integrated the original bill with amendments that were offered.

7. Improved tools for legislators, such as additional staff for major committees, as well as enlarged professional staff for the legislative reference bureau and legislative council; availability of adequate secretarial service on a year-round basis both in Springfield and Chicago; and access to toll-free phone calls to and

from the capitol building and adequate reimbursement of living expenses.

By the time the report was published, the voters had already made a significant change: The Democrats lost control of the Illinois House. Thus, the perfect balance that had existed between the parties ceased to exist, and the Republicans controlled both houses of the legislature. There was concern as to whether a new leadership would be willing to implement the recommendations made in part by those whom they displaced. However, widespread newspaper interest and support of the work of the commission helped to focus attention on the public's expectation of reform. Nevertheless, the recommendation for reducing the number of committees went by the wayside due to the utility of committee chairmanships—the more the better—in a contested race for the speakership.

Then began a struggle within the legislature to bring about changes in the rules of the House of Representatives to incorporate the letter and the spirit of the recommendations. There were strong expressions at times about how the good old days were still as good as ever, about the undesirability of what they called "change for change's sake," about how the commission was trying to "coddle legislators," about how all those notice provisions were unnecessary impediments to efficient operation, since, it was said, all a legislator really needs to do is to follow the advice of his leaders. But in the end, when the rules finally emerged, they incorporated virtually all of the commission's rules recommendations. Deadline scheduling became a reality; minority procedural rights were strengthened; proxy voting in committee was eliminated except for leaders; attention was given to the plugging of loopholes by which committee reference had in the past been frequently bypassed; a new sanctity was given to the House's discharge of its responsibilities in the field of constitutional revision.

AMENDMENTS TO THE CONSTITUTION

Let me discuss another important area of change: amendments to the Illinois Constitution. It was quite apparent that the legislature was haphazard in the way it handled proposed amendments to the state Constitution. They were frequently considered—or ill-considered—at the very height of the end-of-the-session logjam. Procedural requirements relating to notice and passage were less stringent for constitutional amendments than for the most insignificant bill. The new rules incorporated the following changes:

1. Under the new deadline scheduling, the consideration of proposed constitutional amendments was required to be completed prior to the final month of the session. In the commission's words, "we believe that proposed amendments to the Constitution should come before the legislature at a time when the atmosphere is conducive to calm reflection and careful deliberation."

2. New emphasis was required to be given to proposed constitutional amendments by requirements that they be separately grouped in the weekly legislative digest (in the past they had been "lost" amid large numbers of joint resolutions relating to matters of far lesser significance), that they be separately listed on the daily printed calendar (in the past they had not even appeared), and that they be heard, like bills, on three separate days rather than on a single day for final passage.

While we were still experiencing the first blush of enjoyment at the upgrading of the legislature's fulfillment of its responsibilities in amending the Constitution, the following occurred in the wink of an eye. The members of the Illinois House one day found themselves suddenly confronted on the floor with a joint resolution petitioning Congress to call a constitutional convention to revise the Fourteenth Amendment, so as to permit a state to apportion one house on a basis other than population. Quickly, the resolution was adopted by an almost straight party-line vote. Most of us, I am sure, had been unaware that we were engaged in the process of amending the federal Constitution by a then little-known alternate procedure whereby the states can petition Congress to convene a constitutional convention. A few hours later we learned that Illinois had thereby become the thirty-second state to so petition Congress, and that only thirty-four states were required to mandate Congress to call such a convention under this method of amending, which had never before been used. In fact, no one even knows whether such a convention, once legally convened, could prepare amendments to other parts of the Constitution, thereby raising the possibility of a runaway constitutional convention. The floor debate on this resolution was so brief that these points were never even mentioned before a vote was taken.

Investigation revealed that the resolution had been introduced into the House less than twenty-four hours before; committee reference had been bypassed. The network of safeguards we had built into the rules in the field of constitutional revision—notice, committee reference, etc.—had been inapplicable because they applied only to amendments to the *state* Constitution. Anguished cries arose from the various newspapers in the state and from the League of Women Voters over the legislature's having committed Illinois in support of an amendment to the federal Constitution without a chance for public debate or presentation of testimony. Somehow it was not a very impressive answer to the chorus of protests to rejoin, "Y*ou* should complain; we were *in* the legislature, and we didn't even know." Whatever one may think of the substance of the proposal, this kind of procedure demeans the entire legislative process. My immediate response was to file proposals for new rules changes to prevent the recurrence of this kind of legislative anachronism; and I am pleased that these rules changes were eventually adopted with the support of those who sponsored the parliamentary coup.

These events illustrate a significant point: A number of our recommendations were the direct result of unhappy incidents that occurred in our legislature. We would later talk about the problems and how to deal with them intelligently. This stimulated extremely creative discussion in the commission. Instead of merely complaining about shenanigans that are pulled, we need to direct our energies toward establishing procedures that will protect the public interest. In general, I believe that we in the legislative branch can learn much from our brethren in the judicial branch about the importance of regular and orderly procedures, adequate notice, and a fair opportunity to be heard.

THE COMMISSION'S ACHIEVEMENTS

The final report of the Illinois Commission on the Organization of the General Assembly was released in January of 1967. Our legislative session ran from January through June. Of our eighty-seven recommendations, seventy-two were achieved in whole or in part. Among the significant achievements were the convening of a "veto session," accomplished through an adjournment to a September date, rather than the traditional *sine die* adjournment; majority-minority staffing for major committees; deadline scheduling, where the rules set forth a succession of dates by which the significant legislative steps must have been concluded (under the new system the percentage of bills passed in the final week of the session fell from 61 percent in 1965 to 23 percent in 1967); marked improvement in the discharge of the legislative function in the field of constitutional revision; extensive modernization of legislative publications. Subsequently I filed a joint resolution to rescind the legislature's original action. As of this writing, the resolution is pending before the Illinois General Assembly. In the House of Representatives the following was accomplished: Rules were changed to provide seven-day notice of committee hearings instead of twenty-four-hour notice (a similar rule was subsequently adopted in the Senate); proxy voting in committee was eliminated for all but the Speaker; more time was allotted for committee hearings; the bypassing of committees was made more difficult; and the right of a minority to obtain a verification of a roll call was made absolute.

Four years after the Illinois Commission's recommendations were presented, a tabulation showed that forty-five recommendations had been achieved in full, twenty-seven in part, and fifteen not at all. The new Constitution adopted in Illinois in 1970, embodied every proposal for constitutional change made by the Commission.

CONCLUSION

If a joint commission is to be used as a means of bringing about improvement, our format is not the only one to consider. As previously indicated, ours is a bipartisan commission, consisting of an equal number of legislators and public members appointed by the legislative leaders. The Joint Committee on the Organization of Congress consisted solely of legislators. The group in the state of Washington was composed entirely of citizens who reported to a legislative committee. The Citizens Commission on the General Assembly in Maryland, on the other hand, was a completely independent private citizen group. The experience in the various states appears to suggest that an effective job of reorganization and modernization of a legislative body may be achieved under any of the operational formats indicated above. The "ideal" one for any state depends upon the conditions existing at the time in that state. I should say that we in Illinois have found the structure of our commission to work out extremely well; the legislative members and the public members each made significant contributions as a group. Not even an intervening political change could scuttle the movement. The full participation of the legislative leadership in the work of the commission has made it easier, I think, to secure the implementation of the many recommendations, despite a change in the control of the House. Those who will be undertaking such programs in the future should find the reports of the various commissions to be useful in suggesting areas for inquiry, and possible solutions that might be considered. In this regard the Citizens Conference on State Legislatures is an invaluable source of information in this field.

Finally, it seems to be quite essential that in sitting on commissions of this kind, we wear our public hat and not our private hat. As legislators we, of course, have a personal interest in improving our lot. In many instances our personal interest will coincide with the public interest, but advancement of the latter and not the former must always be our motivation. If we become lobbyists for our personal interests, who will be there to protect the public interest? This is not, however, to suggest that the revitalization of the legislative institution can be done well by those who do not believe strongly in the importance of the state legislature in the American constitutional scheme. The sense of historic mission is essential to the success of the project, and our commission, in preparing its recommendations, was not hesitant to suggest that if implemented they could indeed contribute significantly to making certain, in the words of one former member of the Illinois House of Representatives, "that government of the people, by the people, and for the people, shall not perish from the earth."

Strategic Problems
in Legislative Improvement

ALAN ROSENTHAL

In the years ahead, legislatures will probably get better, not worse. There are a number of reasons to believe that legislative improvement, modernization, reform—use whichever term seems most palatable—has not yet run out of steam. The temper of the times favors it. Distrust of executive power and faith in decentralization should give legislatures a larger role than ever before. Revenue-sharing schemes will also stimulate improvement. If state legislatures have to decide how to distribute governmental power and allocate additional monies, they will also have to undergo some significant structural change.

The signs are favorable. Today more state legislatures are trying, and trying harder. Even states with slight reputation for modernism have been bitten by the bug. Mississippi, for example, not only created a legislative study committee but audaciously went north of the Mason-Dixon line to employ a university institute as consultant. In my own state, New Jersey, there is new promise. In the past, the legislature, despite annual sessions of unlimited length, met on the average of only about twenty-seven days a year. In 1970, the New Jersey Senate and Assembly have begun to meet two days instead of only one each week, and legislators may well spend as many as forty days in Trenton during 1970. Surely, if New Jersey can make such an incredible stride forward, legislative improvement must be sweeping every state in the nation.

State legislatures will continue to put together reform packages. What goes into them is extremely important. But my job here is to comment not on the contents but rather on how the brittle ingredients are packed and how the bundle may be delivered with as little breakage as possible. In other words, it is the strategy instead of the substance of institutional improvement to which I shall address this essay. This discussion of strategy, or how to bring reform along, is based on observation of and experience with a number of legislatures during recent years. The points to be made naturally need qualification if they are to apply to specific problems, peculiar people, and current distributions of power and possibilities in any particular state. Recognizing this, I shall nevertheless purposely state strategic problems and principles tendentiously and let the chips fall where they may.

ESTABLISHING AGREEMENT

1. *If legislators cannot agree on the need for improvement in general and certain improvements in particular, nothing much will get done.*

Although legislators can and should fight among themselves about many things, one thing they cannot afford to fight over is legislative improvement. In order to achieve change, and especially to make it work, there has to be a high degree of consensus within the legislature itself.

Disagreement on legislative reform is normal, not exceptional. Legislators naturally oppose change. Like human beings, they are reluctant to abandon the familiar and risk the uncertain. Moreover, there is a feeling among a number of veterans that the new boys have to undergo the same hardships as older members to qualify for admission to the club. "I survived without a secretary, so can he." Others fear that change will redistribute power—as it probably will—and that they may suffer as a consequence. These men, like most of us, are more concerned about what they have personally than what the legislature can have collectively. "Damn the legislature, full speed astern." Some members in many legislatures and many members in some legislatures resist reform, because they fear—and probably rightly so—that they will have to work harder as a result. "As it is now, we devote more energy than we have." Still others frankly disagree on the merits—usually the feasibility—of one proposal or the next. "It won't work, so don't even try."

As if these hurdles are not enough, there is partisanship and factionalism with which to contend. In Wisconsin the failure of a partisan minority and a rigid Speaker to compromise on a proposal to change procedures for appointing standing committees damaged a comprehensive program beyond easy repair. In Rhode Island minority attempts to sock it to the majority did little good as far as legislative improvement was concerned.

2. *Since agreement does not come naturally, it must be nurtured. All members should share in payoffs from an improvement program. Some will share more than others, but allocations cannot be completely lopsided. Individuals, committees, and leadership should all come out ahead.*

A balanced program should allocate benefits equitably. If salary increases, for instance, are tied to other improvements, not only does the legislature stand to gain but so does each individual member. Even without the tangible incentive of salaries, it is possible to offer something for everyone. In Wisconsin, for example, the legislature embarked on an innovative program in professional staffing about six years ago. A fiscal staff was created, primarily to serve the joint finance committee. Caucus staffs were established, to support the leaders and rank-and-file in the two parties of both houses. Legislative interns were recruited from graduate schools, to work with standing committees during the session and with legislative council groups during the interim. Everyone benefited, and for a while everyone was happy.

3. *For those who have very little as well as those who have very much, rewards stemming from legislative improvement may not have to be direct and material. Those who have something that they may lose as a result of change pose a problem. Their suffering should be eased by direct and material benefits.*

The prospect of a stronger, more effective legislature, with individual members possessed of more information and a greater voice, may induce the rank-and-file to support reform. Younger members are not a greedy lot. Our surveys in six states have shown that rank-and-file members are far more likely to favor staff, facilities, and comfort for their leaders and committee chairmen than any booty for themselves. What they do want very often is the opportunity to participate in some meaningful fashion. Legislative improvement can offer the opportunity.

Leaders too can be sold on change, for if they have any skill at all they will be among the principal beneficiaries of a more effective legislature. In some states legislatures are weak and leaders are strong. Under such circumstances, legislative leaders are usually lieutenants for the governor or senior errand boys for state and local party chieftains. They lead the powerless, and in turn are led by the powerful. In many states it need not be so. Jess Unruh as Speaker did much to strengthen the California Assembly and increase the independence of individual members. Yet he managed to maintain control and fashioned a national reputation in the process. Secure leaders can afford to run risks; it is more difficult for insecure ones, but then they have less to lose.

The real sticky business is changing standing committees and challenging committee chairmen. In few states do committees function well. In many legislative bodies there are too many committees. (This is part, but only part, of the problem.) Usually, no more than five or six committees count. Others breathe, but show no additional signs of life. They exist solely to confer the prestige of a chairman's title on those who have supported leaders or to serve as dumping grounds for undesirable bills and unwanted legislators. In Maryland, for example, many members in both the House and the Senate had been assigned to languish in the purgatories of inactive committees. Their morale was low. Within the past few years, the situation changed. The Senate reduced its legislative committees to three and the House cut down to four. Now every legislator may languish—but can also work—on an important committee. Morale is much improved. Surprisingly, the chairmen whose committees were abolished suffered in good grace. They retained most of their perquisites—their secretaries and their offices—which were all they really had to begin with. The leaders survived. In fact, the House Speaker, Marvin Mandel, was elected by the legislature to fill the vacant office of governor —a fitting punishment, perhaps, for reorganizing committees.

Precedent indicates that even the number of committees in a chamber can be reduced. Chairmen may not relish the prospect of having their chairs removed. But indemnity is possible. Not only is there the gratitude of legislative colleagues, but there is the secretary, the desk or office, the subcommittee chairmanship, the assignment to a major committee, and other goodies legislative leaders can offer to compensate for loss.

PARTICIPATION AND IDENTIFICATION

4. *In formulating an improvement program, state legislatures can take a hint from the antipoverty program and emphasize "maximum feasible participation of the poor." By this I simply mean, the greater the participation of legislators, the better.*

Legislatures are not used to formulating programs. They rely on the governor to propose comprehensive programs and on departments, agencies, and interest groups to propose specific ones. But they cannot rely on anyone but themselves to fashion a program for legislative improvement. Only legislators have the experience and motivation to put their houses in order.

5. *One problem is that too few members ever think about the legislature or take into account what it needs.*

Doctors consider themselves doctors; lawyers think of themselves as lawyers. Legislators view themselves as doctors or lawyers, Democrats or Republicans, representatives of a house or senate district, and candidates for Congress, governor, or both. In some states identification by members with the legislature hardly exists. In these places legislatures seldom meet, scarcely work, and exercise almost no independent power. This is the case in New Jersey and until quite recently was true of Connecticut also. In other states, such as California and Florida, members know that they serve in a legislature. They may have outside occupations, partisan affiliations, and private diversions, but they are legislative men nonetheless. In most states institutional awareness and loyalty can stand encouragement.

6. *An effective campaign for legislative improvement will strengthen identification with the legislature, and this—perhaps as much as anything else—will help strengthen the legislature. But such a campaign requires broad, representative, and open involvement by legislators in the formulation of improvement policies.*

One of Eagleton's most important functions in the work we do for state legislatures is essentially therapeutic in nature. We help bring to the surface, and make concrete, feelings that ordinarily are latent. This is done through interviews and discussions with members on topics of legislative reform. Talk sets the stage for improvement, not only because it enables us to gather diagnoses and prescriptions from experienced practitioners, but also because it raises reform as an item on the legislator's agenda. Our presence reminds members that problems do exist, that solutions are possible, and that their views count. Often for the first time, legislators start giving some serious thought to the legislature as an institution.

This is the beginning of involvement, but only that. There has to be activity as well as reflection. A core of members must become solidly committed. Their participation in shaping an improvement program will likely gain their commitment, since effort expended in developing proposals generally creates stakes in having them adopted. Obviously, not everyone can participate if agreement on specific proposals is ever to be reached. But some members must become involved.

Eagleton's career as consultant demonstrates the importance of legislative participation. On starting out, we overlooked the need for continuing consultation with an organized group of legislators. In Rhode Island and Maryland we spoke to many people, fashioned a large number of proposals, and submitted lengthy reports. The results, I suppose, were satisfactory. They would have been far better had legislators played a greater part in the actual formulation of the proposals. In Connecticut the situation was different. A committee of Connecticut leaders met periodically, came up with their own ideas, reviewed and challenged our suggestions, and sent us back to the drawing board repeatedly.

Although not everyone can serve on a legislative study committee, everyone should be kept informed as to the committee's goings on. There is no reason for secretiveness. It will only arouse suspicion, even though there is little worth suspecting. Moreover, there is no reason to sneak a program through, since once it is through it will be up to the entire membership to make it work.

HELP FROM OUTSIDE

7. *It is helpful to encourage outsiders to help the legislature help itself. Some things can be accomplished from within; most depend on support from without.*

In general, whatever a legislature does that requires a constitutional change or costs money is likely to provoke opposition. Changes in rules and procedures or committee reorganization necessitate inside strategies only, but salaries, sessions, and staffing demand strategies involving outsiders as well. These outsiders include citizens groups, the governor, and the press. A legislature certainly cannot afford to have all of them in the enemy camp.

8. *Citizens groups can be extremely supportive, but they must be made to feel that they are accomplishing something, not merely being used.*

How citizens can be of assistance is well illustrated by the contrasting cases of Florida and Connecticut. In the past three years the Florida legislature has done more to improve itself than most legislatures have done in the past twenty. But nearly everything was achieved quietly, without fanfare. There was no attempt to organize citizens or even inform them about progress under way. Recently, after much had already been accomplished, the Florida legislature voted itself a hefty and well-deserved pay raise. It relied on the assurances of the governor that he would sign the bill. Governor Claude Kirk, however, vetoed the bill, castigated the legislature in a special joint session, and then took his case to the people. For Governor Kirk, it was surely his finest hour. The legislature came under the most severe attack. There was at least momentary panic, with nowhere to turn for support. A citizens commission established and participating at a time when the Florida legislature's efforts began, might have made a real difference.

In Connecticut, by contrast, a group organized by the Citizens Conference on State Legislatures has been of substantial help. With a former legislator as co-chairman, the Connecticut group made an independent study, supported many of Eagleton's recommendations, commended the legislature for its efforts, and joined in opposing Governor John Dempsey, who was resistant to legislative change.

9. *A legislature cannot depend on a governor. A governor might remain neutral, but more likely he will oppose anything*

more radical than a consent calendar. A hostile governor, however, may do more to solidify the legislature than the legislature can do to solidify itself.

Governors are natural opponents of legislative modernization. First, many of them are dedicated to the executive-force model of government, conceiving of the legislature as a rubber stamp under the best of circumstances and an obstacle to progress under the worst. A few, such as a former governor of Rhode Island and one or two from New Jersey, regard the legislative branch with some contempt—perhaps with reason. Second, governors feel they have little to gain from improved legislatures, believing with some justification that the stronger the legislature, the weaker the governor. None, I imagine, envy Pat Brown's relationship with Jess Unruh and the California Assembly. Third, governors simply do not want to change arrangements that have proven comfortable in the past. In Connecticut, for instance, legislative improvement threatens the system under which governors, state party chairmen, and local party leaders have continually dominated politics and government. Fourth, an occasional governor will fight the legislature primarily to ride an issue and enhance his own flagging popularity. If I have not been misinformed, this shoe fits Governor Kirk of Florida pretty well.

A legislature can survive gubernatorial hostility, as long as it believes in what it is doing and has a coalition of citizens who share the faith. In fact, an abrasive governor may do more for reform than a well-intentioned legislature. His attacks can engender a sense of institutional identity legislators might otherwise be unable to achieve. In Connecticut the governor vetoed a bill providing for a joint committee on legislative management and several staff agencies. Both houses of the legislature overrode the veto, and by unanimous votes. The battle itself may have a more enduring effect than the important organizational changes at issue.

10. *The real challenge is to wean the press from the governor's breast. This is no easy task.*

Newspaper reporters and editorial writers tend to support the governor. They do not understand the legislature; they do not appreciate the reasons for its untidiness. The hierarchical executive is more comprehensible, warts and all. It is easier to write about, and that which is easier produces nicer reportorial results.

In both Connecticut and Florida the immediate and overwhelming response of the newspaper press was to side with the governor and dump on the legislature. In both states education is proceeding and attitudes may be changing. No startling strategy is involved, but the legislature will have to take the lead. It should take greater pains to inform reporters, even before the balloon bursts, while it is still afloat in the air. Reporters should be told —perhaps by means of backgrounders—what improvements are being considered and why. With sufficient and early explanation, they may begin to understand.

IMPLEMENTING LEGISLATIVE REFORM

11. *It is not just what the legislature proposes to do in the way of improvement that counts; it is also the order in which the legislature proposes to do it.*

Legislators frequently put salaries first, and from their perspectives they are usually justified. In many cases, however, it is difficult to convince the press and public that legislators earn what they get, let alone what they want. Unless the battle is to be bloody, inside priorities will have to be modified to conform to outside ones.

Sometimes this is virtually impossible. There are states where salaries are so low that no legislator in his right mind can be expected to work longer or harder without additional compensation. Rhode Island is one; here salary increases must come before practically anything else. In some states, such as Wisconsin, legislative improvement has been habitual and visible, and voting salary raises is not as tough as elsewhere. In others, such as California, gains in compensation and amenities are always linked to reforms that are highly regarded by the press and public alike.

In some states, despite solid improvement programs, compensation still creates controversy. The problem in Florida was not so much that salaries were put first. Actually, most of the improvement program preceded the salary bill, but the public was not sufficiently aware of this. Had the Florida legislature discussed its past achievements and future plans at the same time it decided on higher salaries—perhaps by means of hearings held by a legislative study committee—it might have met with a less hostile public response. In a few states, and again New Jersey serves as an unfortunate example, the legislature votes a salary increase unaccompanied by any other major proposal for improvement.

The public must be persuaded that salaries are merited because legislators are working longer, harder, and more effectively. This means that other proposals should ordinarily lead off or be featured in a program of legislative reform. The Connecticut legislature seems to be on the right track in this respect. Before voting themselves higher salaries, members decided to go to annual sessions, overhaul their interim operations, modify their rules and procedures, and establish desperately needed research and fiscal staffs.

12. *Once a program is adopted by a legislature, the real struggle begins. Making reforms work so that they accomplish something worthwhile is the most troublesome task of all.*

For most proposals, support must be maintained even after the legislative roll is called. If demobilization is premature, chances are that improvement will abort. Still, there is a definite tendency by all concerned—legislators, consultants, and citizens groups—to concentrate on formulation and adoption, and then leave implementation to a rather dreary fate.

On their parts, legislatures are notoriously deficient in the ability to follow through. They are geared to creating laws, and then abandoning their progeny to the tender mercies of administrators. Oversight or review is woefully neglected. It is not surprising, therefore, that once legislatures formally adopt improvement proposals they regard their products as self-executing. A few are, but others demand continual attention.

Professional staffing is an example of an improvement that requires follow-through. Once the legislature agrees on the need and allocates funds for new or additional staff, the hardest part of the job is still to come. The legislature then faces the difficulties of staff recruitment, compensation, and placement. Once these matters are settled, the legislature still must exercise general control and ensure that the staff is performing as intended. Another example of a reform that is not self-fulfilling is interim work. After a legislature decides that standing committees should operate between sessions, problems of budget, agenda, and coordination will inevitably arise.

Someone must shoulder responsibility for implementing changes that have been adopted. In several states we have recommended the establishment of a joint committee on legislative management, composed of leaders and a few members from each house. Such a group might exercise over-all control of the legislative budget, interim activities, and legislative service agencies.

Much depends not only on legislative leadership but also on legislative staff itself. Staffers can make or break proposed improvements. In some places, such as Wisconsin and Florida, members of the professional staff, under the supervision of leaders, responded positively to changes adopted by the legislature. Implementation, therefore, created no special difficulties. In other places, such as Maryland, a key staff man may be resistant to change; under such circumstances progress will at best be exceedingly slow. Sometimes a legislature has no staff on which to rely for help in implementing reform. Then it must find help. In Connecticut, for instance, the legislature hired as executive director of its newly formed joint committee on legislative management the person who had prepared the report that served as the basis of the reform program. It is ironic justice that the individual mainly responsible for prescribing to the Connecticut legislature is now up against the nitty-gritty of making reform work.

CONCLUSION

Too wide a disparity between expectations about what legislative improvement should do and what it actually does do can lead to frustration and cynicism. Expectations should be realistic; otherwise, results will be disappointing. Legislators, in short, should not convince themselves or others that organizational and structural changes will solve their problems. Their problems will never be solved. The millennium is just that—always a thousand years away. The most comprehensive program—even if *we* recommend it—is unlikely to make a weak legislature strong or a poor legislature good. It may make a weak legislature stronger and a poor one better. Given time and persistence, it may do even more. That is about as much as can reasonably be expected.

BIOGRAPHICAL SKETCHES

ARTHUR BOLTON heads a firm engaged in public policy and management research and consultation. He has worked in the fields of community organization and welfare and mental health. He served as a Senior Consultant and later Director of the Office of Research in the California State Assembly. Mr. Bolton's paper was presented at Eagleton's 1968 conference.

CHARLES O. DAVIS, a partner in a public relations and advertising agency, is executive secretary of the National Conference of State Legislative Leaders. He has had experience as a free-lance writer and newspaper correspondent. Since 1962 he and his agency have been involved in some thirty-five Republican campaigns at all levels in Wisconsin. Mr. Davis's paper was presented at Eagleton's 1970 conference.

DONALD G. HERZBERG is executive director of the Eagleton Institute of Politics and professor of Political Science at Rutgers University. He has served as legislative assistant to a United States senator, administrative deputy director of the Budget Division of the State of New York, and as staff director to the President's Commission on Registration and Voting Participation and the President's Select Commission on Western Hemisphere Immigration. He is chief consultant to the election unit of ABC. His publications include *American Party Politics* (Gerald Pomper, co-author).

HAROLD E. HUGHES, a United States senator since 1969 and a Democratic assistant majority whip, was governor of Iowa from 1963 through 1968. He served as a member of the Executive Committee of the National Governors' Conference and as chairman of the Democratic Governors' Conference. Previously he was a member and chairman of the Iowa State Commerce Commission. Senator Hughes' paper was presented at Eagleton's 1969 conference.

HAROLD A. KATZ has been a Democratic member of the Illinois General Assembly since 1965. During 1966–67 he was chairman of the Commission on the Organization of the General Assembly. Previously, he served as a special consultant to the governor and as master in chancery of the Circuit Court of Cook County.

He has published numerous articles in law journals and other periodicals. Representative Katz's paper was presented at Eagleton's 1967 conference.

WILLIAM J. KEEFE is chairman of the Department and professor of Political Science at the University of Pittsburgh. He is also chairman of the American Political Science Association Congressional Fellowship Program. He has written *The American Legislative Process: Congress and the States* (Morris S. Ogul, co-author), published a number of articles in political science and law journals, and contributed chapters in several books on American politics. Professor Keefe's paper was presented in a slightly different version at Eagleton's 1970 conference.

ROBERT P. KNOWLES has served in the Wisconsin State Senate since 1955, has held the offices of Republican assistant majority leader and majority leader, and is now president pro tempore. He is a member of the Executive Committee of the National Conference of State Legislative Leaders (having earlier been president), is on the Executive Committee of the Council of State Governments, and was appointed by President Nixon to the Advisory Commission on Intergovernmental Relations. In 1964 and 1968 he was executive secretary to the Arrangements Committee of the Republican National Conventions. Senator Knowles' paper was presented at Eagleton's 1967 conference.

WARREN P. KNOWLES served as governor of Wisconsin from 1965 through 1970, having previously held the office of lieutenant governor. A Republican, he was a member of the Wisconsin State Senate from 1941 through 1954, holding the position of floor leader for almost his entire legislative career. He was on the Executive Committee of the National Governors' Conference. Governor Knowles' paper was presented at Eagleton's 1968 conference.

CHARLES F. KURFESS has been Speaker of the Ohio State House of Representatives since 1967 and has been a member of the legislature since 1957. A lawyer and a Republican, he was selected by State House newsmen as the "outstanding freshman representative" during his first term, while the youngest member of the House. He is a member of the Executive Committee of the National Conference of State Legislative Leaders. Representative Kurfess' paper was presented at Eagleton's 1970 conference.

DUANE LOCKARD is chairman of the Department and professor of Politics at Princeton University. He served one term in the

Connecticut State Senate and was a delegate to the New Jersey Constitutional Convention in 1966. He is the author of *New England State Politics, The Politics of State and Local Government, The Governor of New Jersey: A Study in Political Power,* and *Toward Equal Opportunity,* as well as a number of scholarly articles. Professor Lockard's paper was presented at Eagleton's 1966 conference.

LARRY MARGOLIS has been executive director of the Citizens Conference on State Legislatures since 1967. He served for five years as assistant to the Speaker of the California State Assembly. He has worked in political campaigns, community and social service organizations, and in labor unions. Formerly a lecturer in the Department of Political Science at Stanford University, he is currently a visiting lecturer in the Department of Political Science at the University of Kansas. He is a participant in programs of the American Assembly and the American Political Science Association. Mr. Margolis' paper was presented at Eagleton's 1968 conference.

RICHARD B. OGILVIE has been a governor of Illinois since 1969. A Republican, he was elected in 1962 as sheriff of Cook County and in 1966 as president of the Cook County Board of Commissioners. Previously he served as assistant U.S. attorney and as a special assistant to the U.S. attorney general. Governor Ogilvie's paper was presented at Eagleton's 1970 conference.

HOWARD PENNIMAN is professor of Government at Georgetown University. He has held positions as research analyst for the Psychological Strategy Board, chief of the External Research Staff of the Department of State, and chief of the Overseas Publications Division of the United States Information Agency. He served as a delegate to the Maryland State Constitutional Convention. He has written a number of books, including *The American Political Process,* and several articles. Professor Penniman's paper was presented at Eagleton's 1968 conference.

ALAN ROSENTHAL is director of the Center for State Legislative Research and Service of the Eagleton Institute of Politics and a professor of Political Science at Rutgers University. He has written several books as well as a number of scholarly articles. During the past few years, he has directed studies of legislatures in several states. Professor Rosenthal's paper on staff was presented at Eagleton's 1969 conference; his paper on strategies and tactics was presented at a 1969 conference for legislative leaders from the southeastern states.

HOWARD R. SACKS is Dean of the University of Connecticut Law School. He served as a member of the Illinois Conflict of Interest Laws Commission, acted as a consultant to the Association of the Bar of the City of New York in its study of congressional ethics, and has testified on ethics before legislative committees in several states. He was in private practice and federal government from 1948 until 1956, and was then a member of the faculty of Northwestern University Law School until his appointment as Dean of the University of Connecticut Law School in 1967. Dean Sacks' paper was presented at Eagleton's 1968 conference.

CARL E. SANDERS was governor of Georgia from 1963 through 1966. A Democrat, he served previously in the Georgia General Assembly—the House of Representatives during 1955–56 and the Senate during 1957–62. As a state senator, he held the positions of floor leader and president pro tempore. Governor Sanders' paper was presented at a 1969 conference for legislative leaders from the southeastern states.

JESS UNRUH served in the California State Assembly from 1955 through 1970. During that period he held the positions of Democratic majority leader and minority leader. From 1961 until 1970 he was Speaker of the Assembly. He has been President of the National Conference of State Legislative Leaders and a member of the Advisory Commission on Intergovernmental Relations. Mr. Unruh's paper from the leader's position was presented at Eagleton's 1968 conference; his paper on unicameralism was presented at Eagleton's 1970 conference.

SELECTED BIBLIOGRAPHY

This bibliographical section is intended to suggest some of the most relevant publications on important aspects of state legislatures and legislative reform.

On legislative institutions some excellent work has been done. Two major texts—one by William J. Keefe and Morris S. Ogul, the other by Malcolm E. Jewell and Samuel C. Patterson—give broad and intensive coverage to both Congress and state legislatures. The revised edition of Jewell's book on the politics and practices of state legislatures should not be missed. Another major effort is that undertaken by the Twenty-ninth American Assembly on State Legislatures, with background papers prepared by Keefe, Jewell, Duane Lockard, Herbert Jacob, John C. Wahlke, and Alexander Heard for a 1966 conference and published in a volume edited by Heard.

Searching studies of individual legislatures are illustrated by the books of Gilbert Y. Steiner and Samuel K. Gove on Illinois, William C. Havard and Loren P. Beth on Florida, William Buchanan on California, and Lockard on the states of New England. Many things have changed since these authors wrote, but their description and analysis are valuable for an understanding of legislatures today.

Recently the American Political Science Association sponsored the preparation of informative handbooks for legislators in several states. The volumes that resulted—Gove and Richard J. Carlson on Illinois, Ronald D. Hedlund and Wilder Crane, Jr. on Wisconsin, and Charles W. Wiggins on Iowa—give detailed pictures of legislative organization and operations in these states.

Specific aspects of state legislatures have also been examined. On committees there is research by Dean E. Mann, who dealt with the committee system of Arizona, and Alvin D. Sokolow and Richard Brandsma, who dealt with standing committee assignments after reapportionment in California. Articles by James

David Barber on leadership strategies in Connecticut, by Douglas
C. Chaffey comparing legislatures in Montana and Wisconsin,
and by Norman Meller and Alan Rosenthal on legislative staffing
are examples of empirical research that highlight important features of the legislative process. On reapportionment there is the
massive review and analysis from a legal perspective by Robert
G. Dixon, Jr.

The standard work on executive-legislative relations was published some time ago by Coleman B. Ransone, Jr. No study
on the subject is as probing as Roy D. Morey's on the office of
governor in Arizona. Thomas J. Anton's scrutiny of the appropriations process and D. Jay Doubleday's examination of legislative
review of the budget offer a fascinating comparison of legislative
control in Illinois and California. Performance auditing, a technique many legislatures are now attempting to develop, is
thoroughly justified and explained in a book by Lennis M.
Knighton.

Several studies are of lasting theoretical interest. An exploration of the role orientations of legislators in California, New
Jersey, Ohio, and Tennessee by Wahlke and his associates is a
classic. So is Barber's sensitive treatment of the impact of
psychological factors on the recruitment and adjustment of members to legislative life. A comparative analysis of all fifty states
by Wayne L. Francis demonstrates how party competition, apportionment, legislative conflict, patterns of decision making,
and legislative issues and policy outcomes are all interrelated.

Some research, which is now appearing or is about to be
published, also deserve mention. The National Municipal League
has sponsored studies of the impact of reapportionment in ten
states. The Eagleton Institute of Politics has supported studies
of the politics and consequences of legislative change in eight
states, which will soon be available in a volume edited by James
A. Robinson.

Legislative diagnosis and prescription have proceeded at a
rapid pace. Two decades ago the American Political Science
Association set up a committee on American legislatures. After

a four-year study, the committee's report, containing about fifty recommendations, appeared as a volume edited by Belle Zeller. Since then another notable report has been produced, this one by the Committee on Legislative Processes and Procedures of the National Legislative Conference.

Undoubtedly the author with the greatest involvement in a state legislature and the best record at legislative improvement is Jess Unruh. In collaboration with Donald G. Herzberg, he has written a series of essays that suggest and present rationale, programs, and experience in legislative reform.

As part of the activity of the American Assembly, state and regional meetings were held from 1966 through 1968. In preparation, background papers analyzing individual legislatures and proposing specific reforms were drafted. A number of volumes, including ones on legislatures in the Midwest, the Rocky Mountain West, the South, the Southeast, and New England, appeared as a result.

Too numerous to mention are the studies diagnosing legislative ailments and prescribing remedies in particular states. One of the best is the report of the Illinois Commission on the Organization of the General Assembly. Others that merit attention are reports to the Maryland, Minnesota, Utah, and Washington legislatures, prepared either by citizens commissions, legislative committees, or groups composed of both legislators and public members. Recommendations from many reports are reproduced in a compilation issued by the Citizens Conference on State Legislatures.

During the past few years, the Eagleton Institute has also studied state legislatures and made recommendations for their improvement. Published by Rutgers University Press in a series entitled "Strengthening the State Legislature" are separate volumes on Maryland by Rosenthal, on Rhode Island by Charles Tantillo, on Florida by C. Lynwood Smith, on Wisconsin by Alan Chartock and Max Berking, and on Connecticut and Mississippi by David Ogle.

Contemporary information and comparative data on state legislatures and legislative improvement is provided by a number of organizations. The *Book of the States*, published biennially by the Council of State Governments, is the standard source. The Citizens Conference has produced several useful compilations: A *Survey of Legislative Services in the Fifty States*; *State Constitutional Provisions Affecting Legislatures*; and *Compensation for Legislators in the Fifty States*. The Conference's evaluation and ranking of legislatures in all the states was published as a book in 1971.

For the most current information, there are the National Municipal League's *State Legislatures Progress Reporter*, the Council of State Governments' *Legislative Research Checklist* and *The American Legislator*, the National Conference of State Legislative Leaders' *The State Legislative Leader*, and CCSL's Research Memorandums, Spotlights, and Information Bulletins, all of which are issued regularly.

Published books and articles, including those previously mentioned as well as selected others, are listed below alphabetically by author.

ANTON, THOMAS J., *The Politics of State Expenditure in Illinois*. Urbana, Illinois: University of Illinois Press, 1966.

BARBER, JAMES DAVID, *The Lawmakers: Recruitment and Adaptation to Legislative Life*. New Haven, Connecticut: Yale University Press, 1965.

————, "Leadership Strategies for Legislative Party Cohesion," *Journal of Politics*, Vol. 28, May 1966, pp. 347–67.

BOYNTON, G. R., SAMUEL C. PATTERSON, and RONALD D. HEDLUND, "The Structure of Public Support for Legislative Institutions," *Midwest Journal of Political Science*, Vol. 12, May 1968, pp. 163–80.

BUCHANAN, WILLIAM, *Legislative Partisanship: The Deviant Case of California*. Los Angeles: University of California Press, 1963.

CAMPBELL, ERNEST H., ed., *The State Legislatures of Alaska, Oregon, and Washington*. Seattle: University of Washington, 1966.

CANNON, LOU, *Ronnie and Jesse: A Political Odyssey*. Garden City, New York: Doubleday, 1969.

CHAFFEY, DOUGLAS C., "The Institutionalization of State Legislatures: A Comparative Study," *Western Political Quarterly*, Vol. 23, March 1970, pp. 180–96.

CHARTOCK, ALAN and MAX BERKING, *Strengthening the Wisconsin Legislature*. New Brunswick, New Jersey: Rutgers University Press, 1970.

Citizens Commission on the General Assembly, *Reports to the Legislature and the People of Maryland*. The Commission, January 1967.

Citizens Conference on State Legislatures, *Compilation of Recommendations Pertaining to Legislative Improvement in the Fifty States*. Kansas City, Missouri: the Conference, April 1967.

Citizens Conference on State Legislatures, *Selected Bibliography on State Legislatures*. Kansas City, Missouri: the Conference, June 1968.

Citizens Conference on State Legislatures, *State Constitutional Provisions Affecting Legislatures*. Kansas City, Missouri: the Conference, May 1967.

Citizens Conference on State Legislatures (written by John Burns), *The Sometime Governments*. New York: Bantam Books, 1971.

Citizens League Committee on Legislative Organization and Procedures, *Organization for State Policy Making: Twenty-nine Proposals for Strengthening the Minnesota Legislature*. Minneapolis: the League, February 16, 1968.

CLARK, CALVIN W., *Compensation for Legislators in the Fifty States, 1968*. Kansas City, Missouri: Citizens Conference on State Legislatures, October 1968.

———, *A Survey of Legislative Services in the Fifty States*. Kansas City, Missouri: Citizens Conference on State Legislatures, April 1967.

CORNELIUS, WILLIAM G., ed., *Southeastern State Legislatures*. (Alabama, Florida, Georgia, South Carolina.) Atlanta: Emory University, 1967.

Council of State Governments, *Budgeting by the States*. Chicago: the Council, 1967.

Council of State Governments, *Lawmaking in the West: A Summary of Legislative Bill Passing Procedures in Thirteen States*. San Francisco: the Council, 1967.

DISHMAN, ROBERT B. and GEORGE GOODWIN, JR., *State Legislatures in New England Politics*. Durham, New Hampshire: New England Center for Continuing Education, September 10–13, 1967.

DIXON, ROBERT G., JR., *Democratic Representation: Reapportionment in Law and Politics*. New York: Oxford University Press, 1968.

DOUBLEDAY, D. JAY, *Legislative Review of the Budget in California*. Berkeley: Institute of Governmental Studies, University of California, October 1967.

FRANCIS, WAYNE L., *Legislative Issues in the Fifty States: A Comparative Analysis*. Chicago: Rand McNally, 1967.

GOVE, SAMUEL K. and RICHARD J. CARLSON, *An Introduction to the Illinois General Assembly*. State Legislative Service Project, American Political Science Association and Institute of Government and Public Affairs, University of Illinois, December 1968.

HAVARD, WILLIAM C. and LOREN P. BETH, *The Politics of Mis-Representation: Rural-Urban Conflict in the Florida Legislature*. Baton Rouge, Louisiana: Louisiana State University Press, 1962.

HEARD, ALEXANDER, ed., *State Legislatures in American Politics*. Englewood Cliffs, New Jersey: Prentice-Hall, 1966.

HEDLUND, RONALD D. and WILDER Crane, JR., *The Job of the Legislator: Wisconsin*. Washington, D.C.: American Political Science Association, January 1969.

HERZBERG, DONALD G. and JESS UNRUH, *Essays on the State Legislative Process*. New York: Holt, Rinehart and Winston, 1970.

Illinois Commission on the Organization of the General Assembly, *Improving the State Legislature*. Urbana: University of Illinois Press, 1967.

JACOB, HERBERT and KENNETH N. VINES, eds., *Politics in the American States*. Boston: Little, Brown, 1965.

JEWELL, MALCOLM E., *The State Legislature: Politics and Practice*, second edition. New York: Random House, 1969.

JEWELL, MALCOLM E. and LEE S. GREENE, *The Kentucky and Tennessee Legislatures*. Lexington: Department of Political Science, University of Kentucky, 1967.

JEWELL, MALCOLM E. and SAMUEL C. PATTERSON, *The Legislative Process in the United States*. New York: Random House, 1966.

Joint Interim Committee on Facilities and Operations of the Washington State Legislature, *Report to the Legislature on Modernization of State Government*. Olympia, Washington, no date.

KEEFE, WILLIAM J. and MORRIS S. OGUL, *The American Legislative Process: Congress and the States*, second edition. Englewood Cliffs, New Jersey: Prentice-Hall, 1968.

KNIGHTON, LENNIS M., *The Performance Post Audit in State Government*. East Lansing, Michigan: Bureau of Business and Economic Research, Graduate School of Business Administration, Michigan State University, 1967.

LACEY, ALEX B., ed., *Power in American State Legislatures*. (Arkansas, Louisiana, Mississippi, Oklahoma.) New Orleans: Tulane University Press, 1968.

Legislative Study Committeee of the Utah Legislative Council, *Final Report*. Salt Lake City, 1966.

LOCKARD, DUANE, *New England State Politics*. Princeton, New Jersey: Princeton University Press, 1959.

MANN, DEAN E., "The Legislative Committee System in Arizona," *Arizona Review of Business and Public Administration*, Vol. 11, August 1962, pp. 1–10.

MELLER, NORMAN, "Legislative Staff Services: Toxin, Specific, or Placebo for the Legislature's Ills," *Western Political Quarterly*, Vol. 20, June 1967, pp. 381–89.

MOREY, ROY D., *Politics and Legislation: The Office of Governor in Arizona*. Tucson, Arizona: University of Arizona Press, 1965.

National Legislative Conference Committee on Legislative Processes and Procedures, *American State Legislatures in Mid-Twentieth Century: Final Report*. Chicago: Council of State Governments, 1963.

OGLE, DAVID B., *Strengthening the Connecticut Legislature*. New Brunswick, New Jersey: Rutgers University Press, 1970.

———, *Strengthening the Mississippi Legislature*. New Brunswick, New Jersey: Rutgers University Press, 1971.

PATTERSON, SAMUEL C., ed., *Midwest Legislative Politics*. (Iowa, Kansas, Missouri, Nebraska.) Iowa City, Iowa: Institute of Public Affairs, University of Iowa, 1967.

RANSONE, COLEMAN B., JR., *The Office of Governor in the United States*. University, Alabama: University of Alabama Press, 1956.

ROSENTHAL, ALAN, "An Analysis of Institutional Effects: Staffing Legislative Parties in Wisconsin," *Journal of Politics*, Vol. 32, August 1970, pp. 531–62.

————, "Between Sessions—The Effectiveness of Legislative Study and Interim Work," *State Government*, Vol. 44, Spring 1971, pp. 93–101.

————, *Strengthening the Maryland Legislature*. New Brunswick, New Jersey: Rutgers University Press, 1968.

————, *The Interim Work of the Texas Senate*. New Brunswick, New Jersey: Eagleton Institute of Politics, Rutgers University Press, 1971.

SHARKANSKY, IRA, "Agency Requests, Gubernatorial Support and Budget Success in State Legislatures," *American Political Science Review*, Vol. 62, December 1968, pp. 1220–31.

SMITH, C. LYNWOOD, *Strengthening the Florida Legislature*. New Brunswick, New Jersey: Rutgers University Press, 1970.

SOKOLOW, ALVIN D. and RICHARD BRANDSMA, "Leadership Strategy and Legislative Committee Assignments: California after Reapportionment," *Research Reports*, Institute of Governmental Affairs, University of California at Davis, July 1969.

STEINER, GILBERT Y. and SAMUEL K. GOVE, *Legislative Politics in Illinois*. Urbana, Illinois: University of Illinois Press, 1960.

STOIBER, SUSANNE A., ed., *Legislative Politics in the Rocky Mountain West*. (Colorado, New Mexico, Utah, Wyoming.) Boulder, Colorado: Bureau of Governmental Research and Service, University of Colorado, 1967.

TANTILLO, CHARLES, *Strengthening the Rhode Island Legislature*. New Brunswick, New Jersey: Rutgers University Press, 1968.

WAHLKE, JOHN C., HEINZ EULAU, WILLIAM BUCHANAN, and LEROY C. FERGUSON, *The Legislative System*. New York: Wiley, 1962.

WIGGINS, CHARLES W., *The Iowa Lawmaker*. Ames, Iowa: Iowa State University, no date.

ZEIGLER, HARMON and MICHAEL A. BAER, *Lobbying: Interaction and Influence in American State Legislatures*. Belmont, California: Wadsworth, 1969.

ZELLER, BELLE, ed., *American State Legislatures*. New York: Thomas Y. Crowell, 1954.

INDEX